AMERICAN
REVOLUTION

Signaling horn

Tea chest

Snuff box

Regimental coat

Poster by Paul Revere

"Brown Bess" musket

Drum

Continental money

Loading the cannon

DK EYEWITNESS BOOKS

AMERICAN REVOLUTION

Written by
Stuart Murray

Telescope

Candle lantern

In Association with the
Smithsonian Institution

Stoneware jug

LONDON, NEW YORK, MUNICH,
MELBOURNE, and DELHI

MEDIA PROJECTS INC.
Executive Editor C. Carter Smith
Managing Editor Carter Smith
Project Editor Aaron Murray
Designer Laura Smyth
Photo Researchers Robyn Bissette (S.I.), Athena Angelos

DK PUBLISHING
Editor Beth Sutinis
Senior Art Editor Michelle Baxter
Creative Director Tina Vaughan
Jacket Art Director Dirk Kaufman
Publisher Andrew Berkhut
Production Manager Chris Avgherinos

First American Edition, 2002
4 6 8 10 9 7 5
Published in the United States
by DK Publishing, Inc.
375 Hudson Street,
New York, New York 10014

Continental infantryman

DK Publishing, Inc. offers special discounts for bulk purchases
for sales promotions or premiums. Specific, large-quantity needs
can be met with special editions, including personalized
covers, excerpts of existing guides, and corporate imprints.
For more information, contact
Special Markets Department, DK Publishing, Inc.

Library of Congress Cataloging-in-Publication Data
Murray, Stuart, 1948-
        American Revolution / by Stuart Murray.
        American Revolution.—1st American ed.
                p. cm. — (Dorling Kindersley eyewitness books)
        Written in association with the Smithsonian Institution.
        Summary: A visual guide, accompanied by text, to the people,
battles, and events of America's war for independence.
        ISBN 0-7894-8556-7 — ISBN 0-7894-8557-5 (lib. bdg.)
        1. United States—History—Revolution, 1775-1783—Juvenile
literature. [1. United States—History—Revolution, 1775-1783.] I. Dorling
Kindersley Publishing, Inc. II. Smithsonian Institution. III. Series.

E208 .A427 2002
973.3—dc21
                                                                    2001047619

Reproduced by Colourscan, Singapore
Printed in China by Toppan Printing Co., (Shenzhen) Ltd.

see our complete product line at
www.dk.com

Regimental flag

Pipe tomahawk

Colonial doll

Liberty cap weathervane

Purple heart

Contents

George Washington's sword and scabbard

Life in British America

After the French war ended in 1763, peace and prosperity came to the Thirteen Colonies, which had profited from supplying the empire's military efforts. There were more than 2,700,000 colonists by 1775, and Philadelphia (population: 30,000) was a leading city in the British Empire. The ports of New York, Boston, and Charleston were booming, too, but most people lived on family farms, and agricultural products were the main export. There was little industry, so manufactured goods, such as textiles, hats, and ironware, were imported from Britain. Each colony elected its own law-making assembly and had its own governor—most governors were appointed by the king. Many colonies printed their own currency to promote buying and selling of goods and services. The colonials were proud to be British subjects, but for years they had been left alone to manage their own affairs. Now at peace with France and in possession of Canada, the British government intended to keep the growing American colonies under strict control.

Map labels

MASSACHUSETTS (MAINE)
NEW HAMPSHIRE
Salem
Boston
NEW YORK
MASSACHUSETTS
RHODE ISLAND
Newport
CONNECTICUT
PENNSYLVANIA
New York
Philadelphia
NEW JERSEY
Baltimore
Annapolis
DELAWARE
MARYLAND
Charlottesville
VIRGINIA
Atlantic Ocean
NORTH CAROLINA
SOUTH CAROLINA
Charleston
GEORGIA
Savannah
APPALACHIAN MOUNTAINS

The Thirteen Colonies
- Settlement growth in 1660
- Settlement growth in 1700
- Settlement growth in 1760

THE THIRTEEN COLONIES
The American colonies that rose up against British rule lay along the Atlantic seaboard; territories occupied by European and African populations are shown for 1660 (dark green), 1700 (lighter green), and 1760 (lightest green).

New England Colonies

The four northeastern colonies—Massachusetts, Connecticut, Rhode Island, and New Hampshire—relied on farming, seafaring, fishing, and shipbuilding. Boston was the major seaport, with Newport, Rhode Island, growing fast. The unsettled region known as Maine was important for great trees, which were used as ship masts. New England had many free laborers, as well as skilled artisans such as carpenters, printers, tailors, wig makers, shoemakers, and goldsmiths. There were few slaves.

FREEDOM SUIT
Young men often bound themselves to a tradesman for seven years as an apprentice to learn a skill. At the end, they might receive new clothes, a "Freedom Suit," such as this one from Rhode Island.

A CAPTAIN'S DIARY
New England sailors and ships were highly regarded around the world; Captain Ashley Bowen of Marblehead, Massachusetts, recorded voyages and drew pictures of ships in his diary.

THE CENTER OF THE HOME
A colonial family in Malden, Massachusetts, gathered in this kitchen for meals and prayers, or sat before the hearth at night to do handiwork, mending, spinning, and repair of tools and leather goods.

The Middle Colonies

New York, New Jersey, Pennsylvania, and Delaware had two large cities: Philadelphia and New York. Most people lived on small farms, but Philadelphia was one of the empire's largest cities, bustling with trade and commerce. Philadelphia was rich in colonial culture, such as music and art. New York, with its fine harbor, was one of the busiest ports in the empire and was also a center of trade with native peoples.

A New Jersey eighteen pence note, issued in 1776

THE STATE HOUSE
The colonial government of Pennsylvania met in Philadelphia at the State House, built between 1732–41, and one of the handsomest buildings in America.

QUAKER FARM
This prosperous 18th-century Pennsylvania farm is a bustling scene in summertime, with the farm family and hired hands plowing fields and managing horses and other livestock; in 1775, most colonials lived on farms, large and small.

The Southern Colonies

Most white people in Maryland, Virginia, North Carolina, South Carolina, and Georgia lived on family farms, but large-scale plantations dominated the economic and social systems. To produce cash crops—mainly tobacco, indigo, and rice—for market, the plantations relied on the forced labor of thousands of field slaves. Virginia, alone, had 200,000 African-American and African-born slaves, almost half the total population. The South's two largest towns were Charleston and Baltimore.

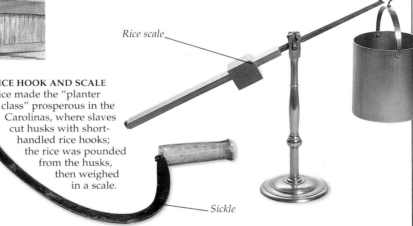

Rice scale

RICE HOOK AND SCALE
Rice made the "planter class" prosperous in the Carolinas, where slaves cut husks with short-handled rice hooks; the rice was pounded from the husks, then weighed in a scale.

Sickle

VIRGINIA'S CAPITAL
Rivaling Philadelphia in political influence, but not in size, Virginia's capital, Williamsburg, boasted its own magnificent government building.

SLAVE QUARTERS
Slave families on large Southern plantations sometimes lived in cabins, but often were crowded together in large barracks where there was little privacy; food was usually cooked on fires outside their quarters.

War in the New World

WHENEVER FRANCE AND ENGLAND were at war, their American colonies also fought. The great Seven Years' War of 1754–63 was a worldwide struggle on land and sea between the two mightiest empires. In America, it was called the French and Indian War, with the outnumbered French and their Native allies fighting the numerous British colonists and Redcoat soldiers sent over from Britain. In previous years, American campaigns involved small forces, but now the armies numbered in the thousands. A new generation of Americans, including the Virginian George Washington, gained valuable military experience in this war. At first, the French won major battles, defeating Edward Braddock in 1755, but the French strongholds fell, one by one, and fortresses such as Quebec became British possessions. With the coming of peace, there would still be Indian uprisings, such as Pontiac's Rebellion, but the American colonies were strong and prosperous as never before.

GRAND STRATEGIST
William Pitt, 1st Earl of Chatham, was Britain's prime minister during most of the Seven Years' War, and planned strategy for the campaigns that captured French Canada.

CANADA
N.H.
MA.
N.Y.
R.I.
PA.
CT.
N.J.
DE.
VA.
MD.
N.C.
S.C.
GA.
FLORIDA

European Colonial Holdings
- ☐ British
- ☐ French
- ☐ Spanish

BRITAIN'S AMERICAN EMPIRE
Victory in the French and Indian War broke French power in America and brought vast areas of eastern North America into the growing empire of English King George III; the colonies now were ready to expand westward.

Young Washington

Troops from Virginia were led by militia colonel George Washington. While traveling through the hills and forests of western Pennsylvania and the Ohio Valley, Washington had to write many reports for headquarters. Though just 26 years of age, he rose to command a British brigade, the only American-born officer to reach such a high rank during the war.

Colonel George Washington, c.1772

Officer's writing set used on campaign

SLAUGHTER ON BRADDOCK'S ROAD
An arrogant commander in chie who knew nothing of wilderne fighting, British general Edward Braddock led an army of 1,400 Redcoats and colonials against the French and Indians defending Fort Duquesne in Jul 1755. Braddock's army was ambushed and almost wiped out, except that young George Washington organized the retreat of the survivors. The nearly 1,000 British and colonia casualties included Braddock, who was buried under the road that was given his name.

FALL OF QUEBEC
The last great stronghold of the French army in Canada, Quebec City stood high above the Saint Lawrence River, seemingly impossible to attack from water level. In September 1759, British troops under General James Wolfe rowed ashore to climb the cliffs by an undefended track, then defeated the French under the Marquis de Montcalm. Both commanders died in the battle.

ENDURING MEMENTOS
Hundreds of British and French cannonballs littered battlefields of the French and Indian War; these were found at Fort Ticonderoga, a French-built bastion on Lake Champlain that was abandoned to the British in 1759.

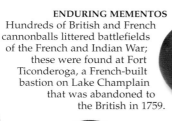

"King's Arrow," also called "Broad Arrow," says cannonball is royal property

French cannonball with royal fleur-de-lis symbol

Pontiac's Rebellion
Some native peoples who had fought alongside the defeated French refused to accept British rule after the French and Indian War. Led by Ottawa chief Pontiac, several nations attacked British garrisons in May 1763 and laid siege to Fort Detroit. Warriors also struck at the colonial frontier, burning cabins and driving out thousands of settlers. British and colonial troops soon invaded and, after hard fighting, forced the nations to make peace in 1766.

REGIMENTAL COAT
This British uniform coat was worn by Major John [I]ngworthy, an officer in the [4]4th Regiment of Foot, which fought during the French and Indian War.

Pipe tomahawk, used both for smoking and war-making

RETURN OF PRISONERS
In Pontiac's Rebellion, warriors unexpectedly rose up against the British, who had taken over the French outposts in what was called the Old Northwest. Indian war parties captured many settlers before the uprising was finally defeated. Victorious British commander Colonel Henry Bouquet met with leading chiefs of the Shawnee and Delaware nations to arrange for the return of their captives.

Taxation without representation

IN THE 1760S, THE BRITISH PARLIAMENT placed new taxes on the colonies. The 1764 Sugar Act, the 1765 Stamp Act, and the 1767 Townshend Acts put taxes and duties (fees) on imports such as sugar and tea and on printed documents and publications. Many Americans objected, claiming that only their colonial legislatures had the right to tax them. Since colonies did not elect representatives to Parliament, these acts were illegal "taxation without representation." Angry colonists resisted, refusing to import British goods until the acts were lifted; government officials were violently attacked to prevent tax collection. In 1768, 4,000 Redcoats occupied Boston to punish the city for its resistance, and conflicts erupted between Bostonian and soldiers. The worst clash was the "Boston Massacre" of 1770, when Redcoats fired on a threatening mob. Three years later, anti-Parliament leader Samuel Adams organized a group of men who boarded a merchant ship and dumped its tea cargo into Boston harbor.

"No Stamp Act"

A Virginia family's teapot made it clear they opposed the 1765 Stamp Act that required all legal documents and printed paper to have revenue stamps; such stamps were kept in this leather box marked "GR," meaning "George, Rex," or "King George."

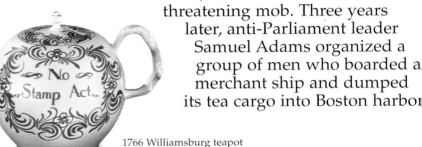

1766 Williamsburg teapot

"GR" for "George, Rex"

Tax collector's box

Revenue stamps

THE BOSTON TEA PARTY
Several ships carrying imported tea were attacke by colonial protesters, but the most celebrated "tea party" was on December 1 1773, when locals disguise as Indians threw 342 tea chests into Boston harbor.

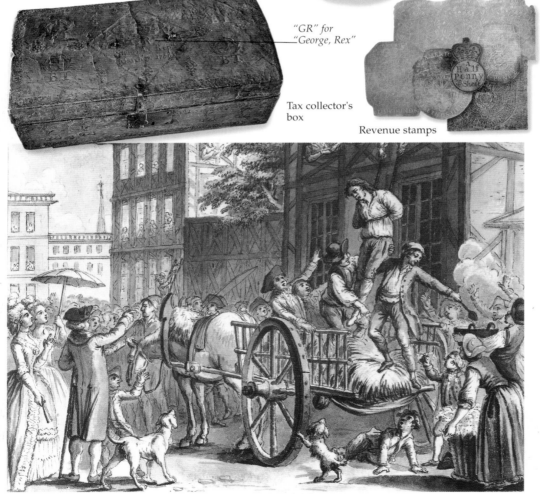

TARRED AND FEATHERED
Radical Bostonians attack a government tax collector, coating him with hot, sticky tar and covering him with feathers.

The Boston Massacre

Conflict between Bostonians and Redcoats flared into violence in 1770, when soldiers on guard duty were harassed by a rowdy mob. Some enraged Redcoats fired, killing five people. Put on trial, the soldiers were defended by respected attorney John Adams, who won acquittals for most, and for others only light punishment.

SAMUEL ADAMS
Massachusetts radical Samuel Adams was one of the most outspoken opponents of Parliament's taxation of the colonies; he was among the first to consider total independence from Britain.

COFFINS FOR VICTIMS
This period engraving laments the Boston Massacre, showing coffins inscribed with initials of the dead. "C.J.A." is for Crispus Attucks, the first African-American killed in the Revolution.

FIERY PROPAGANDA
A poster by engraver Paul Revere depicts troops at the Boston Massacre firing together on command, which was not the case.

TEA CHEST
Tea grown in the Far East was shipped in stout boxes to America, where it was popular until colonists stopped drinking it to protest British import duties. This is a miniature replica of one of the East Indian tea boxes said to have been thrown into Boston Harbor.

The Revolution's opposing leaders

KING GEORGE III WANTED REBELLIOUS AMERICA HUMBLED once and for all. With the king's support, Prime Minister Lord North led the government's military efforts to bring the colonies under control. Some British statesmen and generals, such as Member of Parliament Edmund Burke, believed armed conflict would be a disaster for the empire. Another Englishman who hoped to avoid full-scale war was Sir William Howe, a general who had made America his home for 20 years. The leading colonial military figure was Virginia's George Washington, chosen to be commander in chief of the armies of Congress. New England patriots John Adams and John Hancock were among the first delegates to the Continental Congress. Adams was a political theorist, while Hancock was a wealthy merchant who became president of Congress. New York's John Jay, a skilled legal mind, also became a president of Congress. Along with Adams, Jay later traveled to France to represent America in international affairs.

EMBLEM OF ROYALTY
The coat of arms of the British royal house features a lion and a unicorn and the symbols of England, Scotland, Wales, and Ireland.

LORD FREDERICK NORTH
Prime Minister North led politicians who wanted to tax the colonies. North allied himself with King George, opposing men such as Edmund Burke, who objected to Britain's colonial policies.

SIR WILLIAM HOWE
A lifelong soldier who spent most of his military career in America, General Howe did not agree with British colonial policies. Yet, he was a dutiful soldier, and took command of the British army in North America in 1775.

PROCLAMATION OF REBELLION
In 1775, King George's royal proclamation declared the American colonies to be in rebellion. Many colonists, he said, had forgotten the allegiance "they owe to the power that has protected and supported them."

THE BRITISH SOVEREIGN
In the full glory of his coronation robes, King George III was just 22 when he took the throne in 1760. Americans first objected to British laws by petitioning the king to support the colonies' position, but he refused. George was determined to keep the colonies obedient to England.

The American commander in chief

The Second Continental Congress appointed George Washington commander of all its forces because he was the patriot with the most military experience. Washington swore always to obey Congress because he believed the military must never take the reins of power in a republic. Washington refused to become directly involved in politics while he was a soldier.

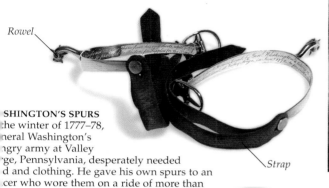

WASHINGTON'S SPURS
In the winter of 1777–78, General Washington's hungry army at Valley Forge, Pennsylvania, desperately needed food and clothing. He gave his own spurs to an officer who wore them on a ride of more than ... miles to Boston to arrange for supplies.

Rowel

Strap

AT HOME IN VIRGINIA
Washington was a masterful horseman with a powerful physique. These attributes combined with his wisdom and courage to help him endure eight years as commander in chief. He is pictured at his beloved Mount Vernon plantation in Virginia. Washington left home at the start of the Revolution and did not return again for six years.

THE FIRST SIGNER
Since Boston patriot John Hancock was a smuggler who avoided Parliament's port fees, the British tried hard to arrest him. Hancock eluded capture and later became president of the First and Second Continental Congresses. He was the first to sign the Declaration of Independence.

A POLITICAL MASTERMIND
Lawyer John Adams of Massachusetts was an early challenger to British colonial policy. A leading delegate to the Continental Congress, Adams nominated Washington as commander in chief. After helping draft the Declaration of Independence, Adams served in France as representative for the United States.

A BRITON FOR AMERICA
Edmund Burke called, unsuccessfully, for Parliament to negotiate with the American colonies, rather than make war. He also championed the rights of other British colonies, including India, and tried to ease government oppression of Ireland, where he had been born.

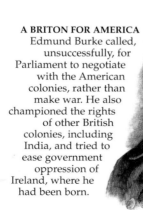

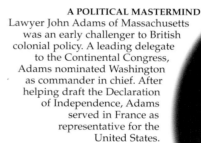

JOHN JAY
A brilliant New York attorney and jurist, Jay served as a delegate to the Continental Congress and later was an important diplomat. Recognized for his ability in legal matters, Jay was president of Congress from 1778-79. Soon afterwards he joined the American peace commission in Paris.

PENNSYLVANIA COAT OF ARMS
The newly independent states had to create their own official coats of arms. Pennsylvania's shows a ship, a plow, and sheaves of wheat along with an eagle and two white horses.

Unrest becomes revolution

To punish Massachusetts for the Boston Tea Party, Parliament voted in 1774 to place harsh regulations on the colony. These were called the "Intolerable Acts" because the colonies would not tolerate them, or the "Coercive Acts" because Britain was coercing, or bullying, America. These acts closed the port of Boston until the tea was paid for, and limited Massachusetts's rights to rule itself. Farmers, artisans, and merchants from other colonies sent money and food to help Boston, and a "continental congress" was held in Philadelphia. This First Continental Congress united the colonies to stop buying British goods until Parliament repealed the Intolerable Acts. American men, women, and children organized at home to manufacture goods to replace British imports, and a Second Continental Congress was planned for 1775 if Britain did not change its policies. Meanwhile, Benjamin Franklin was returning to Philadelphia from London. He then believed the colonies must resist by force of arms.

PATRICK HENRY
A radical Virginia legislator, Henry believed King George had no right to rule America; calling for the colony to prepare for war, Henry declared, "Give me liberty or give me death."

The Raleigh Tavern

In 1774, the Virginia legislators, or burgesses, prepared to vote against the Coercive Acts, but the royal governor refused to let them meet in the Williamsburg statehouse; instead, they moved to nearby Raleigh Tavern, named for English adventurer Sir Walter Raleigh—misspelled "Ralegh" on its signboard. They agreed to boycott British goods, arm the colony, and send delegates to the First Continental Congress in Philadelphia.

Raleigh Tavern's signboard

Snuff box

A TAVERN'S PEWTER WARE
Many colonial tavern items, from drinking mugs, called "tankards," to plates and small boxes, were made of pewter, which was tin combined with lead, brass, or copper.

Pewter tankard

Preparing for conflict

The colonies armed to resist British oppression, and gunsmiths turned out muskets as fast as they could. These were called "flintlocks," because pulling the trigger caused a flint to strike a spark and fire the bullet. Firearms and ammunition were secretly stored in remote barns and buildings where the king's soldiers could not get at them. By early 1775, many Americans were ready to fight if the British kept suppressing colonial freedom.

Musket flints

Paper cartridge holds a bullet and gunpowder

FREEDOM'S FORGE
American gunsmiths were skilled at manufacturing long-barreled hunting rifles, but soldiers needed short muskets that could take a bayonet. Also, the musket could be loaded more quickly than the rifle. Rapid firing and bayonet charges by massed troops were essential to the success of an 18th-century army.

SPINNING AND WEAVING FOR LIBERTY
To defy Parliament, Patriot women mobilized to spin thread and weave cloth that would replace fabric normally imported from the British Empire. During the resistance period, women worked to make the colonies more self-sufficient. They often called themselves "Daughters of Liberty."

Portrait of Franklin

Publisher, scientist, statesman

Benjamin Franklin was a Philadelphia author and publisher, known for his experiments with electricity. Early in his career, Franklin moved briefly to England, where he worked as a printer. He later returned to London as a colonial representative. In 1775, after trying unsuccessfully to reach a settlement between Parliament and the colonists, he came back to America, expecting an armed struggle.

Franklin ran this press in a London printshop.

"JOIN OR DIE"
Franklin created this sketch showing the individual American colonies as a snake that is cut into pieces; in order for the snake—and the colonies—to survive, the parts must unite to work together.

Continued from previous page

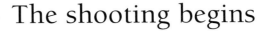

The shooting begins

On the night of April 18, 1775, General Thomas Gage ordered Redcoats to search for colonial military suppli[es] being stockpiled in Concord. Patriot leader Dr. Joseph Warren sent out riders, including silversmith Paul Rev[ere] and tanner William Dawes, to alert the militia. The nex[t] day, British soldiers and Lexington militiamen fired o[n] each other. The Redcoats marched on to Concord, but militia forced them to retreat. The Americans laid sieg[e to] Boston—and the Revolution began.

"ONE IF BY LAND, TWO IF BY SEA"
One of two candle lanterns placed in the spire of Boston['s] Old North Church on the night of April 18, 1775, to aler[t] militiamen that Redcoats were crossing to the mainlan[d] by boat. Only one lantern would have meant the British were moving by land, two meant by wate[r.]

Statue cast in bronze

THE RIDE OF PAUL REVERE
Revere was part of a Patriot network organized to warn of any British military activity. His mission was to alert leaders John Hancock and Samuel Adams in Lexington. They escaped just as the first Redcoats arrived to arrest them.

MILITIA CANTEEN
A soldier needs water, which was carried by Connecticut militia lieutenant Joseph Babcock in this wooden canteen. Babcock, whose initials are carved into the canteen, responded to the "Lexington Alarm" in April 1775.

Shoulder strap for carrying canteen

THE MINUTEMAN
This statue by sculptor Daniel Chester French honors the Massachusetts militiamen of 1775, who left their plows to muster instantly against Redcoats marching out of Boston.

LEXINGTON GREEN
British major John Pitcairn shouted "Disperse, ye rebels!" at defiant Minutemen gathered on Lexington Green, and a moment later firing broke out. The Revolution had begun. The artist, Amos Doolittle of Connecticut, visited this site soon after the clash.

A BLOODY RETREAT
After reaching Concord, the Redcoats found themselves surrounded by thousands of armed and angry militia. The march back to Boston, 20 miles away, became a fierce, running battle all through the day. From behind trees, houses, and stone walls, militiamen fired at the troops, who burned houses along the way and often counterattacked.

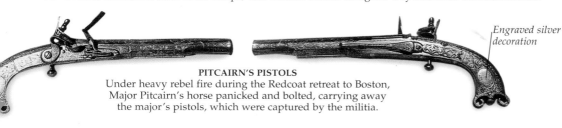

Engraved silver decoration

PITCAIRN'S PISTOLS
Under heavy rebel fire during the Redcoat retreat to Boston, Major Pitcairn's horse panicked and bolted, carrying away the major's pistols, which were captured by the militia.

Capture of Fort Ticonderoga

Once-mighty "Fort Ti" was in poor repair in 1775 and occupied by only a few British soldiers, but it controlled strategic Lake Champlain. The garrison did not expect an American attack when it was awakened on May 10 by yelling rebels under the command of leaders Ethan Allen and Benedict Arnold. The helpless British commander, Captain William Delaplace, was ordered to surrender or die—he surrendered.

ETHAN ALLEN'S COMPASS
His sundial compass helped Green Mountain Boys leader Ethan Allen find the way to Fort Ticonderoga; the fort's capture was joyfully announced in a printed broadside distributed in New York and New England.

British commander, Captain William Delaplace

Ethan Allen demands the surrender of Fort Ticonderoga.

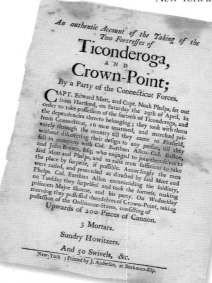

An authentic Account of the Taking of the Two Fortresses of
Ticonderoga,
AND
Crown-Point;
By a Party of the Connecticut Forces.

CAPT. Edward Mott, and Capt. Noah Phelps, set out from Hartford, on Saturday the 29th of April, in order to take possession of the fortress of Ticonderoga, and the dependencies thereto belonging; they took with them from Connecticut, 16 men unarmed, and marched privately through the country till they came to Pittsfield, without discovering their design to any person, till they fell in company with Col. Earthun Allen. Col. Easton, and John Brown, Esq; who engaged to join themselves to said Mott and Phelps, and to raise men sufficient to take the place by surprise, if possible. Accordingly the men were raised, and proceeded as directed by said Mott and Phelps. Col. Earthun Allen commanding the men, on Tuesday they surprised and took the fortress, making prisoners Major Skeene, and his party. On Wednesday morning they possessed themselves of Crown-Point, taking possession of the Ordinance-Stores, consisting of
Upwards of 200 Pieces of Cannon.
3 Mortars.
Sundry Howitzers.
And 50 Swivels, &c.
New-York : Printed by J. Anderson, at Beekman-Slip.

Broadside announces taking of Fort Ticonderoga

Breed's Hill and the siege of Boston

UNDER COVER OF DARKNESS ON JUNE 16, 1775, hundreds of American militiamen dug fortifications on Breed's Hill, on the Charles Town peninsula, across the Charles River from Boston. The orders were to take nearby Bunker Hill, but rebel general Israel Putnam mistakenly seized Breed's instead. The next day, General Gage's Redcoat regiments rowed across to the attack as their artillery fired on the Americans. The British were pushed back twice before driving out the rebels, but more than 1,000 Redcoats were killed and wounded, compared to 500 rebel casualties. Two weeks later, General George Washington arrived to take command of the siege. The British government was angry about such heavy Redcoat losses, and in October replaced Gage with General William Howe. Late that winter, American artillery officer Henry Knox brought captured cannon to Washington, who soon aimed them at Boston. Faced with this threat, Howe had no choice but to evacuate the city, using every vessel he could find. On March 17, after the Redcoats and thousands of Loyalist civilians had sailed away, Washington's troops marched triumphantly into Boston.

CHARLES TOWN BURNS, REDCOATS ATTACK
British artillery in Boston and warships fire red-hot cannon into Charles Town, setting it ablaze. Redcoats disembark f boats and form up in ranks f assault on the rebels entrench at the top of Breed's Hill.

PRESCOTT CALMS HIS MEN
British artillery fired cannon balls into the entrenchments on Breed's Hill. When a man was killed, Colonel William Prescott leaped into the open, defying the fire. Prescott's men kept working in spite of the artillery.

THOMAS GAGE
General Gage was commander of British troops in the colonies. Married to an American, Gage had tried to avoid bloodshed, but after Lexington and Concord his army was trapped in Boston by thousands of angry rebel militiamen.

ATTACK ON BREED'S HILL
The Redcoats were twice driven back by the American defenders, who finally were overrun by a third British assault. Among the American dead was Dr. Joseph Warren; among the British was Major Pitcairn of the Royal Marines.

CHARLES TOWN

British ships

WASHINGTON REVIEWS HIS TROOPS
General George Washington took command of the rebel army besieging Boston and soon built strong defenses to prevent the British from attacking. The Redcoats also were well fortified, however, and it seemed Washington's army could never drive them out.

Silver lion head pommel

Ivory grip

PUTNAM'S SWORD
Patriot general Israel Putnam, a leader at the siege of Boston, owned this sword. It could have served as a weapon for combat or as a dress sword for formal occasions.

Steel blade, 27 inches long

REBEL GUNS COME TO BOSTON
In the winter of 1775–76, Henry Knox and his men dragged, pushed, floated, and carted 59 heavy guns more than 300 miles to Boston. The artillery came from captured Fort Ticonderoga on Lake Champlain. It weighed 60 tons and included mortars like this one, which could fire explosive shells high into the air and drop them onto a target.

Opening 8 inches wide

Bronze mortar barrel weighs 700 pounds

YANKEE POWDER HORN
Soldiers kept gunpowder in hollowed-out horns that they often decorated with carved pictures. This horn was carried by Connecticut soldier Frederick Robbins during the siege of Boston. Carvings show rebels in camp, drilling with muskets and swords.

"In Defence of Liberty" is carved into horn

221 feet tall

Statue of rebel officer Colonel William Prescott

THE BRITISH EVACUATE BOSTON
With rebel guns preparing to bombard the city, British General Howe ordered his army and the Loyalists to depart by ship. Before leaving, Howe's men destroyed what military supplies they could not take and threw some heavy cannon into the bay to prevent the Americans from getting them.

THE "BUNKER HILL" MONUMENT
In 1825, the people of Boston erected a monument to the battle at Breed's Hill. Visitors can climb the 294 steps of this obelisk (four-sided stone pillar) for a view of the city.

Recruiting and training

IN 1775, MANY AMERICANS WERE members of militia companies—mainly social clubs that met a couple of times a year on "training days." When the Revolution started, men turned out with local militia for a short term of service, sometimes only a few weeks. This was not enough time to train and organize a fighting force to meet the king's professional soldiers, who were much better supplied and equipped. The states and Congress soon established regiments that enlisted men for much longer terms. These volunteers were taught military basics so they could maneuver on the battlefield, and some became excellent artillerymen. Their officers usually learned from drill manuals created for the rebel army. At first, there were few uniforms, so most men wore civilian clothes, broad-brimmed hats, and homespun shirts. With strict discipline and training, American soldiers were able to stand up against the Redcoats and earned their respect.

THE DRUMMER
A company's drummer rapped out rat-tat-tat beats that told men to get up, to fall into ranks, when to eat, when to fetch water, wood, and more. In battle, drummers beat commands so officers could control the movements of troops.

PRIDE OF THE MUSICIAN
An American carried this drum throughout the Revolution. Drums had to be well cared for so they could send loud signals to the troops over the din of battle.

FIRST RECRUITS FOR THE REVOLUTION
As friends and family look on, officers teach unskilled volunteers in civilian clothes how to handle muskets while standing in rank. By 1779, the best American regiments had uniforms and knew how to march. In later battles, these troops moved swiftly in well-disciplined formations that impressed both their French allies and British enemies.

Equipping the recruit

[Mi]litia carried their own firearms, while the regiments of [th]e states and Congress used government-issue weapons. If [a] man had money—which few did—he could buy his own [e]quipment. Congress and the states were unable to pay [th]eir troops, who usually suffered [fr]om lack of supplies. Most [so]ldiers had to make their own [b]ullets, using a pliers-type [b]ullet mold that formed [le]ad into balls.

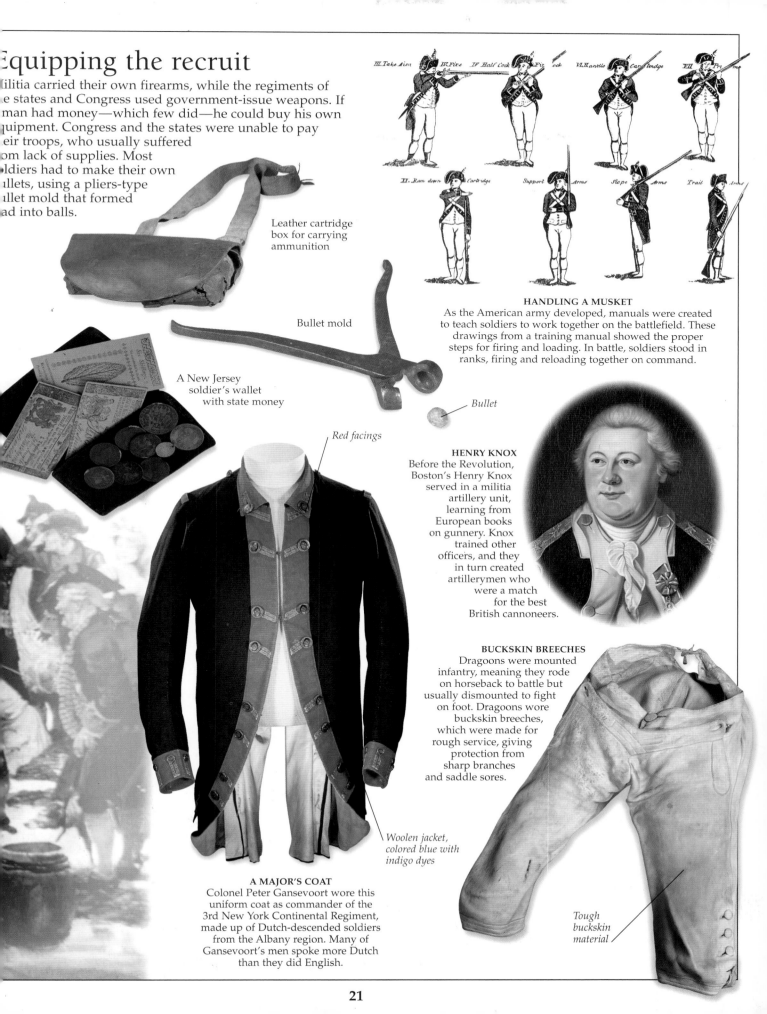

Leather cartridge box for carrying ammunition

Bullet mold

A New Jersey soldier's wallet with state money

Red facings

Bullet

HANDLING A MUSKET
As the American army developed, manuals were created to teach soldiers to work together on the battlefield. These drawings from a training manual showed the proper steps for firing and loading. In battle, soldiers stood in ranks, firing and reloading together on command.

HENRY KNOX
Before the Revolution, Boston's Henry Knox served in a militia artillery unit, learning from European books on gunnery. Knox trained other officers, and they in turn created artillerymen who were a match for the best British cannoneers.

BUCKSKIN BREECHES
Dragoons were mounted infantry, meaning they rode on horseback to battle but usually dismounted to fight on foot. Dragoons wore buckskin breeches, which were made for rough service, giving protection from sharp branches and saddle sores.

Woolen jacket, colored blue with indigo dyes

Tough buckskin material

A MAJOR'S COAT
Colonel Peter Gansevoort wore this uniform coat as commander of the 3rd New York Continental Regiment, made up of Dutch-descended soldiers from the Albany region. Many of Gansevoort's men spoke more Dutch than they did English.

The armies of King and Congress

IN 1775, THE BRITISH ARMY was one of the best in the world. Nicknamed "Redcoats" because of their red uniform jackets, they came from England, Scotland, Ireland, and Wales. They were joined by thousands of blue- or green-coated German soldiers hired from the states of Hesse and Brunswick and termed "Hessians." American Loyalists also formed fighting units, usually wearing green coats. The American revolutionary army was made up of "Continentals"—regiments raised by the Continental Congress—and regiments belonging to the states. Also, civilian militia often left their homes to fight for the Revolution when the war swept into their region. Continentals usually wore blue or brown coats, while state regiments, riflemen, and militia volunteers mostly wore civilian clothes or hunting shirts. Continental and British infantry carried smoothbore muskets and used the same basic battle tactics: massed firing by ranks and charging with the bayonet.

REGIMENTAL NUMBER
This badge decorated a leather cartridge box carri... by a British soldier of th... 26th Regiment of Foot.

BRITISH GRENADIER
Each regiment had a grenadier company—men trained to throw grenades. By 1775, these companies were the elite troops, distinguished by their tall hats, as seen on this 57th Regiment grenadier.

The Loyalists

A third of the American population remained loyal to Britain, and thousands of "Loyalists" fought as the king's troops. British officer Banastre Tarleton created a Loyalist cavalry legion that was the best mounted force of the British army in America. Another notable unit was the 84th Royal Highland Emigrant Regiment, made up of Scottish colonists who opposed the Revolution.

84th Royal Highland Emigrant Regiment camp flag

Tarleton's Legion cavalryman

TRIUMPHANT OCCUPATION
Perfectly drilled companies of Redcoats and thei... German allies parade through New York City while mounted officers and civilians look on; the city was captured by the king's forces in th... summer of 1776, and garrisoned by Redcoats, German troops, and Loyalists throughout the rest of the war.

PHILADELPHIA LIGHT HORSE FLAG
A distinguished Revolutionary unit was the Philadelphia Light Horse, made up of men from leading Pennsylvania families; the troop served throughout the war as a valuable scouting force for Washington's army.

"Brown Bess" musket

THE CONTINENTAL LINE
The Continental infantryman, or "line soldier," was the heart of the Revolutionary army, trained to stand firmly in rank during the heat of battle.

EVOLUTIONARY HAT
...erican colonists usually wore "old-...ioned" three-corner cocked hats, ...orns, while the latest British style ...s the two-cornered bicorn.

DRUMBEAT OF DISCIPLINE
The American army became more effective as its men learned to march, form up in ranks, and behave like disciplined soldiers; the drum and fife set the rhythm for troops on the march and sounded out commands and signals that could be heard across the battlefield.

...rtillery
...merican artillerymen were essential to ...e success of the revolutionary forces. ...rges from New England to Virginia ...de cannon and shot, but American ...nners were always short of equipment ...d ammunition. They often used guns ...d gear supplied by their French allies ...d reused British cannon balls picked up ...ring battles. Respected for their outstanding ...curacy and skill, rebel gunners helped win ...y battles in the Revolution.

Artillery gauge shows the angle at which the cannon barrel must be placed to hit a given target

Shell for explosive

"King's Arrow," states that cannonball is royal property

REBEL GUN CREW
A well-trained crew could swiftly load, aim, and fire; these artillerymen swab their gun's hot muzzle with a damp sponge to eliminate sparks before reloading.

Early Northern battles

LATE IN 1775, AMERICANS MARCHED against the Canadian towns of Montreal and Quebec to prevent the British Navy from landing a powerful force there. Led by New York generals Philip Schuyler and Richard Montgomery, the expedition captured Montreal in November, then moved against Quebec. Another expedition—commanded by Benedict Arnold of Connecticut—crossed the Maine wilderness in a brutal march to join them. The combined American force was defeated at Quebec, however, and Montgomery killed. In spring of 1776, a British army arrived at Quebec by ship, drove the Americans out, then invaded southward over Lake Champlain. Arnold hurriedly built gunboats to challenge the much larger British fleet at Valcour Island. His vessels fought gallantly, but were defeated. Still, such resistance made the British worry about being caught in the open by the approach of winter. Instead of continuing the invasion, they withdrew to Canada, planning to return in 1777.

THE TAKING OF ETHAN ALLEN
During the American campaign to capture Montreal in late 1775, a for of New England volunteers under Ethan Allen was trapped by Briti and Canadians who charged out and took them prisoner.

Montgomery's officer's sash

EARLIEST TROPH
The flag of the British Seventh Regiment of Foot was the first ever captured by an American force; it was won in 1775 at the fall of Fort Chambly in Canada

EARLY BATTLES IN THE NORTH
Early clashes occurred in the Lake Champlain-Hudson River corridor—the main route of travel between Canada and New York. Dotted lines indicate colonial borders.

MONTGOMERY FALLS
American brigadier general Richard Montgomery was struck by cannon fire in the failed assault on Quebec on December 31, 1775; the second-in-command was Colonel Benedict Arnold, shown arriving at right, who would be wounded in the defeat.

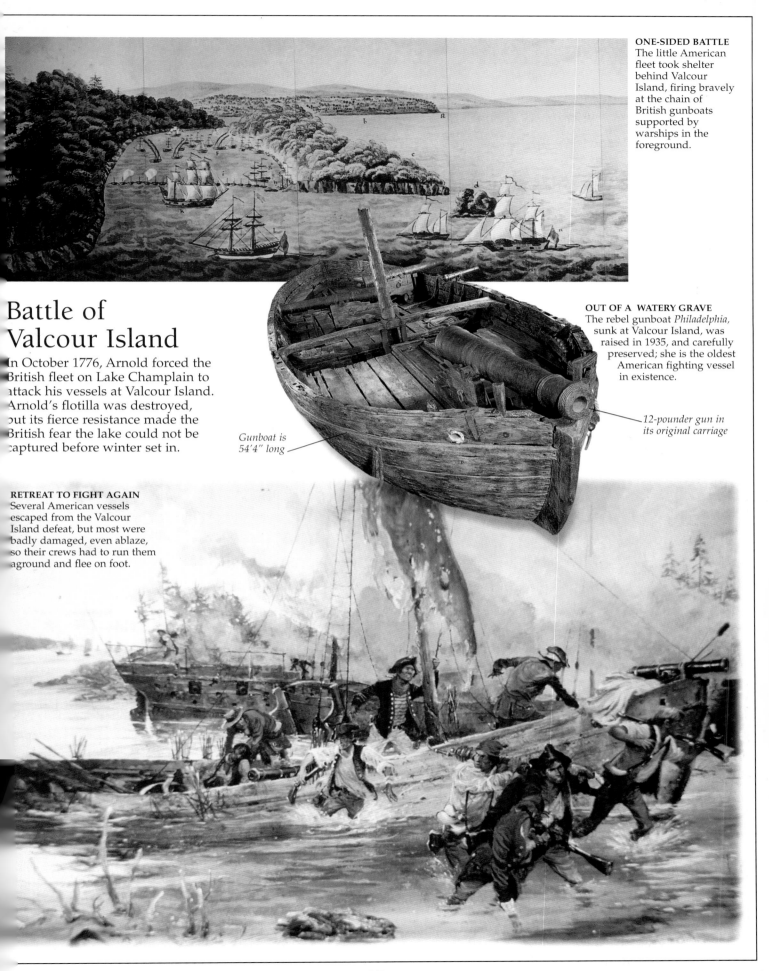

Battle of Valcour Island

In October 1776, Arnold forced the British fleet on Lake Champlain to attack his vessels at Valcour Island. Arnold's flotilla was destroyed, but its fierce resistance made the British fear the lake could not be captured before winter set in.

OUT OF A WATERY GRAVE
The rebel gunboat *Philadelphia*, sunk at Valcour Island, was raised in 1935, and carefully preserved; she is the oldest American fighting vessel in existence.

12-pounder gun in its original carriage

Gunboat is 54'4" long

RETREAT TO FIGHT AGAIN
Several American vessels escaped from the Valcour Island defeat, but most were badly damaged, even ablaze, so their crews had to run them aground and flee on foot.

The Declaration of Independence

IN JUNE 1776, THE COLONIES were ready for independence, but an official document was needed to set out the reasons for separating from England. The Second Continental Congress, which met in Philadelphia, established a five-member drafting committee to write the document. Thomas Jefferson composed the first draft for the committee to work on. By that time, thousands of Americans were inspired by patriot Thomas Paine's pamphlet *Common Sense*, which said "A government of our own is our natural right," and Jefferson agreed. When the document was presented to Congress, it contained a list of complaints against Great Britain, including objections to troops being sent to the colonies and the levying of taxes without American consent. The 56 delegates hotly debated the final wording until July 4, when Congress unanimously adopted the Declaration of Independence. The formal copy of the Declaration was ready for signing in August, and John Hancock, president of Congress, boldly wrote his name largest of all.

THOMAS JEFFERSON
The 33-year-old Jefferson drafted the Declaration of Independence for Congress. An excellent writer, he tried to create an inspiring document that would convince the colonists to unite as one nation.

Drawer for papers, pens and inkwell

JEFFERSON'S DESK
Far from his home and office in Virginia, Jefferson used this folding portable writing desk to draft the Declaration. The work required many solitary hours of thinking, after which he returned to his desk to compose. The small drawer holds writing implements such as quills and ink.

THE LABOR OF LIBERTY
Benjamin Franklin, left, and John Adams, center, members of the Declaration drafting committee, helped Jefferson, right, prepare the document. Discarded pages littered the floor as the men worked on the momentous words that would declare the colonies to be independent states.

COMMON SENSE
In 1776, Thomas Paine's 50-page pamphlet *Common Sense* stirred up American determination for liberty, asserting that government was intended to serve the people and foster their happiness, not oppress them. He said, "the last cord is now broken" between America and Britain.

COMMON SENSE;
ADDRESSED TO THE
INHABITANTS
OF
A M E R I C A,

On the following interesting
S U B J E C T S.

I. Of the Origin and Design of Government in general, with concise Remarks on the English Constitution.

II. Of Monarchy and Hereditary Succession.

III. Thoughts on the present State of American Affairs.

IV. Of the present Ability of America, with some miscellaneous Reflections.

Man knows no Master save creating HEAVEN,
Or those whom choice and common good ordain.
THOMSON.

PHILADELPHIA;
Printed, and Sold, by R. BELL, in Third-Street.
MDCCLXXVI.

PRESENTING THE DECLARATION TO CONGRESS
On July 1, 1776, the five members of the Declaration of Independence drafting committee formally presented their finished document to Congress's president John Hancock, seated; the committeemen were, from the left, Adams, Roger Sherman of Connecticut, Robert Livingston of New York, Jefferson, and Franklin. This painting was done several years later by artist John Trumbull.

THE ASSEMBLY ROOM
The chamber in Independence Hall, in Philadelphia where Congress met to approve the Declaration, was much smaller than suggested by John Trumbull's painting. President Hancock sat at the center rear, and the delegates were at tables around the room.

CONGRESS'S INKSTAND
Delegates used the quills of this silver inkstand to sign the Declaration.

John Hancock's signature

THE DECLARATION OF INDEPENDENCE
Signed by delegates from all the states, the Declaration of Independence bore the heading, "In Congress, July 4, 1776," with the subhead, "The unanimous Declaration of the thirteen United States of America."

Battles and campaigns

A̲FTER W̲ASHINGTON FORCED S̲IR W̲ILLIAM H̲OWE to evacuate Boston in the spring of 1776, the British looked for another place to attack. Howe soon sent a small expedition against Charleston, South Carolina, but was repulsed. Next, he landed an enormous invasion force near New York and advanced across Lon̲ Island to defeat Washington's army. Outnumbered more than two to one, the Patriots regrouped but were defeated again and again. Washington had to retreat across New Jersey, then over the Delaware River into Pennsylvania. It seemed Philadelphia would soon fall to the British. However, on Christmas Eve, Washington counterattacked, routing a detachment of German troops at Trenton, and a few days later he defeated a British force at Princeton. The Patriot army marched to Morristown in the New Jersey hills, where it would remain camped for the winter. The British victories at New York seemed less decisive now that Washington had struck back.

BULLET MOLD
Soldiers made ammunition using molds such as this one carved from soapstone. The two halves of the mold were fastened together and molten lead poured into the channels leading to the hollow forms. When the lead cooled, the mold was opened to reveal musket balls.

A failed British attack

British commander Sir Henry Clinton led a fleet of nine warships and 2,500 Redcoats against Charleston in June 1776. Clinton landed troops to attack the fort on Sullivan's Island, which guarded the harbor, but the Redcoats were forced back. Then the fort's guns so pounded the warships that the invasion was called off, and Charleston saved. The fort was named Fort Moultrie in honor of its commander, Colonel William Moultrie.

CHARLESTON'S DEFENDE̲
South Carolina's Colonel William Moultrie (1730–180̲ was the hero of the Sullivan̲ Island engagement in 1776̲ Moultrie had only 21 guns̲ against the overwhelming firepower of ten enemy warships, but his men fired more accurately than the British.

THE BATTLE OF LONG ISLAND

In August 1776, Sir William Howe landed 32,000 troops close to New York City. Howe sent 20,000 soldiers against Washington's 8,000-man army, which was fortified on Long Island. The Patriots were defeated and trapped against the East River, but under cover of darkness Washington evacuated his army to Manhattan island.

Steel blade,
5 3/4 inches long

A SOLDIER'S RAZOR

Beards were unfashionable among Revolutionary soldiers of both armies. When not on the march, the men used straight razors to keep their faces clean-shaven.

Grenade design

AMERICAN GRENADIER CAP

Like the British, some Patriot troops wore tall caps that indicated they were in an elite company called grenadiers. This cap belonged to a soldier of the 26th Continental Infantry Regiment, which fought at Trenton in 1776.

RISING FROM DEFEAT

Driven from New York in 1776, Washington's army retreated across the Delaware River. On Christmas Day, he gambled everything by crossing back over the ice-choked river and surprising German soldiers at Trenton. The victory stunned the British high command, who realized the war was not yet over.

A SECOND STUNNING BLOW

Early in January 1777, the aggressive British general, Lord Cornwallis, came after Washington to avenge the Trenton defeat, but his quarry slipped away in the night. Washington's 5,200-man army immediately struck at Cornwallis's rear-guard in Princeton, inflicting casualties of 400 killed, wounded, or captured. Only 40 patriots were killed or wounded.

Continued from previous page

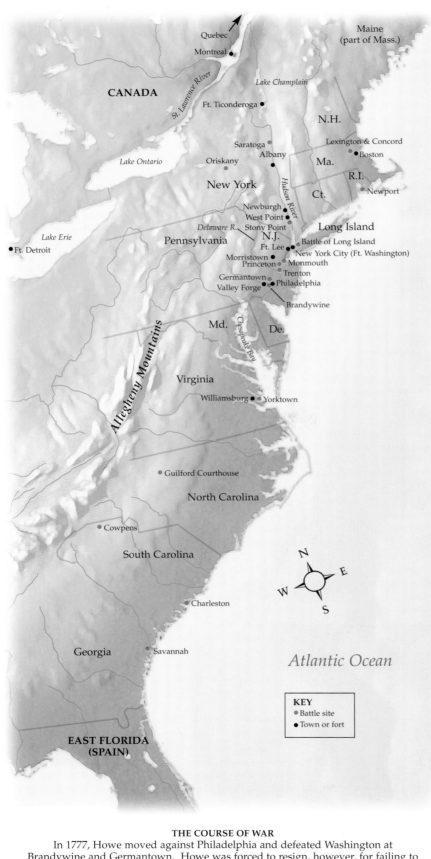

THE COURSE OF WAR

In 1777, Howe moved against Philadelphia and defeated Washington at Brandywine and Germantown. Howe was forced to resign, however, for failing to destroy Washington's army. Howe was also faulted for not supporting Burgoyne, who was captured at Saratoga. The new British commander, Sir Henry Clinton, abandoned Philadelphia in mid-1778 and returned to New York. Clinton then shifted the main theater of action to the South in the hope of pacifying that region.

The greatest battles

In August 1777, Sir William Howe landed 15,000 British troops near Philadelphia and met Washington's army of 10,500 at Brandywine Creek. Howe triumphed and took possession of Philadelphia. Yet, the re army remained intact. In September, Washington attacked British encampments Germantown, Pennsylvania. The assault drove the enemy back, but American inexperience allowed a British counteratta to win the day. There was hope for the Revolutionary cause, however, as Burgoyn was captured at Saratoga in October. Duri the following winter of 1777–78 at Valley Forge, Washington's men were drilled in battlefield maneuvers until they were accomplished soldiers. By summer, they w ready to attack the new enemy commande Sir Henry Clinton, who had replaced How Clinton abandoned Philadelphia, sending army across New Jersey toward New York Washington attacked him at Monmouth, a the battle ended a draw. Washington next moved his army to the Hudson Valley to continue the siege of New York City.

Halberd

Iron spontoons

Wooden sh

LETHAL POLE
Spontoons were symbols of rank also weapons for combat. At first, sergeants carried ha and officers carried spontoons, or half-pike time, halberds were rep by more effective swords muskets with bayonets.

ATTACKING THE CHEW HOUSE AT GERMANTOWN
The first American assaults at Germantown drove the enemy back until 120 Redcoats made a stand in a stone house belonging to the Chew family. The Americans could not capture the house and their advance was held up. Then, confusion in heavy fog caused some Americans to fire on each other, resulting in panic, and Washington's army retreated.

ANTHONY WAYNE (1745–96)
Wayne was an aggressive Continental commander, known as "Mad Anthony" because of his reckless spirit. A Pennsylvanian, he fought in Canada and in the Philadelphia and Monmouth campaigns of 1777–78. He won fame in 1779 for storming Stony Point on the Hudson.

DANIEL MORGAN (1736–1802)
A frontier leader, General Morgan served against Burgoyne and Howe in the battles of 1777–78. He was a skillful commander of sharpshooting riflemen. Morgan's great victory was destroying a force of 1,100 in 1781 at Cowpens, South Carolina.

Touch hole

"Brown Bess" musket

Brush

Pick

Touch hole pick and brush

A BRITISH "BROWN BESS"
The Redcoat musket was named for the brownish color of its barrel. A "Brown Bess" fired a .75-caliber lead ball, accurate to about 75 yards. The soldier carried a pick and brush to clean black powder residue that clogged the touch hole, which had to be clear for the spark to ignite the charge.

The Battle of Monmouth

As Clinton's army of 10,000 men left Philadelphia in June 1778, Washington decided to attack it. He sent General Charles Lee with 6,400 men to begin the action, but Lee lacked confidence and retreated when Clinton's brigades turned to face him. Washington, with 7,000 men, appeared at the crucial moment to stop the retreat. Furious with Lee, Washington took command and beat back several British assaults. Each side lost about 360 men. The Redcoats held the battlefield but withdrew in the night, heading for New York City. Monmouth was the last major battle in the North.

MOLLY PITCHER FIGHTS AT MONMOUTH
Women who carried water for their men in battle were given the nickname "Molly Pitcher." The most famous Molly was Mary Ludwig Hays, whose husband—a Pennsylvania artilleryman—fell wounded at Monmouth. Mary took his place, and after the battle, Washington, himself, commended her bravery.

WASHINGTON STOPS LEE'S RETREAT
As General Lee rode back with his division in full retreat, Washington arrived and angrily demanded to know why. Lee, a former British dragoon officer, claimed his men could not stand against such a formidable enemy. Washington exploded in anger, sent Lee to the rear, and hurried his troops into battle order. Lee was court-martialed and suspended from duty.

Victory at Saratoga

A ROYAL ARMY SET OUT FROM CANADA in June 1777, journeying over Lake Champlain in hundreds of vessels, large and small. Commanded by English general John Burgoyne, the force numbered about 7,000, including Redcoats, Germans, loyalist Americans who opposed the Revolution, and a few hundred Indian warriors. Burgoyne aimed to capture Albany, New York, and join up with the British army operating around New York City. In July, he captured Fort Ticonderoga. The British force advanced slowly down the Hudson River north of Albany, but in August part of the army was defeated near Bennington, Vermont. In October, after a month of fierce fighting at Saratoga, Burgoyne's entire force was defeated and captured. This battle was the turning point in the Revolution, convincing France that the American cause was worth supporting.

A CORRIDOR OF WAR
The Lake Champlain-Hudson River region had long been a strategic military zone; Burgoyne thought he could divide New England from the rest of the colonies by capturing it.

JOHN BURGOYNE
The dashing General Burgoyne won the confidence of King George III, who placed him in command of the royal Northern Army for the 1777 campaign; Burgoyne underestimated the strength of the American opposition, which surrounded and captured his expedition at Saratoga, New York.

American sharpshooter

General Simon Fraser is shot

THE FALL OF GENERAL FRASER
The most experienced British officer at Saratoga was General Simon Fraser, who was killed by an American sharpshooter firing from high in a tree. Fraser had served in the colonies through the French and Indian War and was much loved by his men; he often argued against Burgoyne's misguided plans, but the overconfident commander ignored him.

SHARPSHOOTING RIFLE

The most accurate firearm of the day, rifles were used by rangers and sharpshooters in both armies; the rifle was loaded with a measure of black powder poured into the barrel, followed by a lead ball pushed in with a wooden starter and forced all the way down with a ramrod.

Ramrod

Rifle ball starter

Powder measure

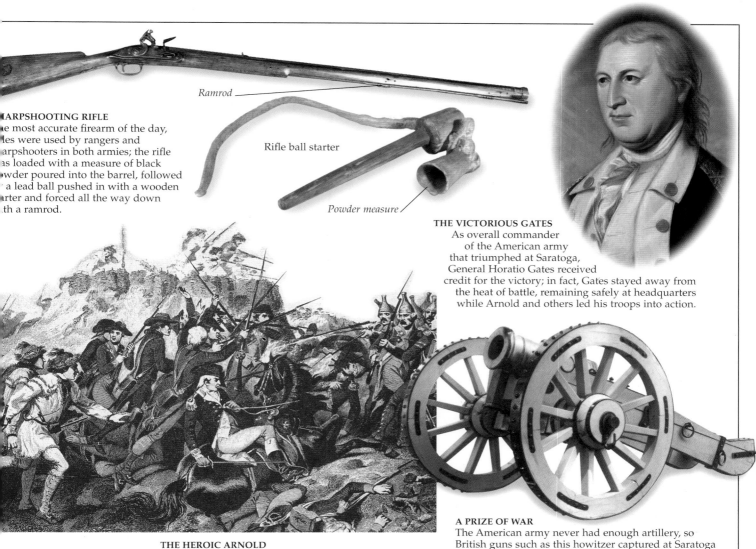

THE VICTORIOUS GATES

As overall commander of the American army that triumphed at Saratoga, General Horatio Gates received credit for the victory; in fact, Gates stayed away from the heat of battle, remaining safely at headquarters while Arnold and others led his troops into action.

THE HEROIC ARNOLD

Before Benedict Arnold betrayed the cause of Revolution and joined the British, he was one of the best American generals; leading a successful assault against German defenders during the Saratoga fighting, Arnold was shot from his horse and severely wounded in the leg.

A PRIZE OF WAR

The American army never had enough artillery, so British guns such as this howitzer captured at Saratoga were often sent to other troops who needed them; this cannon was inscribed by its captors with the proud words: "Surrendered by the Convention of Saratoga, October 17, 1777."

REDCOAT KETTLE DRUM

Each British regiment had a corps of musicians that led the way on marches and in parades, and in battle set instruments aside to carry wounded men; this kettle drum of the Ninth Regiment of Foot—the Royal Norfolk Regiment—was captured by the Americans at Saratoga.

BURGOYNE OFFERS HIS SWORD IN DEFEAT

At the Saratoga surrender ceremonies, General Gates receives Burgoyne, who offers his sword to the victor; at right, American officers look on, with royal officers at left. Following military tradition, Gates only touched the sword, then allowed Burgoyne to keep it as a sign of respect for a gallant, though defeated, opponent. Burgoyne was able to have the surrender terms called a "convention," or agreement, rather than an unconditional surrender.

Attacks on the frontier

JOSEPH BRANT (1742–1807)
Called Thayendanega by his Iroquois people, Brant was a Loyalist during the Revolution. Educated in a Connecticut Indian school, he became secretary to the British superintendent of Indian affairs and later commanded Iroquois forces fighting patriots on the New York frontier.

NATIVE PEOPLES WERE CAUGHT between the British and the Continental Congress during the Revolution. Indians feared a Patriot triumph would lead to mass white migration into their lands, so most tribes remained loyal to Great Britain. Hoping the king would defend them, approximately 13,000 warriors fought for the British, only a few hundred for the rebels, and thousands more remained neutral. Vicious fighting between whites and Indians raged along the frontiers, from New York to Georgia. Early in the war, loyal Indians in the South were defeated by Patriot forces, but in New York's Mohawk Valley, Iroquois under Chief Joseph Brant joined loyal whites and Redcoats to raid Patriot strongholds year after year. Armed by the British, warriors from the Northwest Kentucky, Ohio, Indiana, and Illinois attacked frontier settlements and farms. Led by George Rogers Clark, Virginia frontiersmen invaded the Northwest in 1778–79, capturing the British governor and reducing attacks from that region.

GIFTS OF HONOR
Gorgets were decorated plates worn at the throat by army officers to indicate rank. Some were given by colonial governments to honor native chiefs. The silver gorget with a neck strap is believed to have belonged to Iroquois Joseph Brant.

SLAUGHTER AT ORISKANY
In 1777, an army of British, Loyalists, and Iroquois invaded New York from Canada, advancing along the Mohawk River. They attacked Fort Stanwix, which refused to surrender. Militiamen hurrying to aid Stanwix were ambushed at Oriskany by Iroquois led by war chief Joseph Brant. The militiamen retreated, but a fresh Patriot force caused the invaders to withdraw, and Stanwix was saved.

The daring Long Knives

Patriot frontiersmen of Kentucky and western Virginia were nicknamed "Long Knives" because they carried extremely large hunting knives. Throughout the Revolution, their scouting parties fought bitterly against Loyalist Indian nations. In 1778, 200 Long Knives led by George Rogers Clark journeyed into the wilderness of the Old Northwest—Ohio, Illinois, and Indiana—to surprise important British trading posts. Clark captured forts at Vincennes and Kaskaskia and made a prisoner of Redcoat commander, Lieutenant Colonel Henry Hamilton. As a result, the British Army held only Fort Detroit in the Northwest.

GEORGE ROGERS CLARK (1752–1818)
This Virginia frontiersman was an explorer and surveyor in the Ohio Valley and Kentucky when the Revolution began. Clark commanded the region's Patriot militia, which defended Northwest settlements against Loyalist raiders and their Indian allies. In 1778, he led a force into Illinois territory and captured key enemy forts.

Cowhorn

Rawhide strap for carrying

POWDER HORN
Precious black gunpowder used in the frontier long rifle was kept safe and dry in hollowed-out cow horns that were sealed with carved wooden plugs and slung on rawhide thongs. Even in wet wilderness conditions, powder horns were effective in protecting gunpowder.

THE AMERICAN RIFLEMAN
The frontier rifleman was physically tough and knew forest fighting as well as any Indian warrior. He wore a fringed hunting shirt and leggins and carried a tomahawk and long-bladed knife. Respected as sharpshooters and scouts, riflemen roved the forest paths to protect settlements and watch for enemy war parties. Frontiersmen often ambushed the enemy and were ambushed in turn.

Round-brimmed hat with feather

Hunting knife

Iron blade

Long rifle

Leggins protect legs and feet

HUNTING KNIFE
Frontiersmen depended on a good knife for skinning game, preparing food, and for close-in fighting. This long blade has a handle made of antler.

TERMS OF SURRENDER
By marching 20 flags back and forth behind thickets and beating on drums, Clark tricked Hamilton into believing a powerful Patriot force surrounded the fort. Hamilton soon agreed to sign Clark's articles of surrender.

FORT SACKVILLE FALLS TO CLARK
In his 1778–79 campaign, Colonel George Rogers led a grueling winter march to capture Fort Sackville at Vincennes, on the Wabash River. British commander Henry Hamilton surrendered the post to Clark, assuring Patriot control of a vast frontier region that included the future Indiana and Illinois.

Winter soldier

WHEN COLD WEATHER CAME, American forces in northern climates had to survive the bitter conditions. Although both armies usually stayed in quarters during the worst weather, Washington was always on the alert for a surprise enemy attack. In the winter of 1778–79, his little army was weak and hungry when it went into camp at Valley Forge, Pennsylvania. By spring, however, it emerged as a solid fighting force. This was thanks to former Prussian officer Baron Friedrich von Steuben, who for months trained officers and men in essential battlefield drills. Yet, winter quarters were more than just a time for drilling and trying to keep warm. Since the army usually had a different camp each year, the men had to build log huts and shelters for livestock, equipment, and supplies. At Morristown, New Jersey, for example, Washington's army required more than 1,200 buildings for its encampment.

BARON FRIEDRICH VON STEUBEN
A soldier in his native Prussia, Von Steuben joined Washington's army at Valley Forge and organized a system of drilling troops. This Prussian nobleman trained a group of officers who, in turn, taught their own men what they had learned.

VON STEUBEN'S MANUAL
Baron Von Steuben wrote a drill manual, *Regulations for the Order and Discipline of the Troops of the United States,* which was used to train the entire American army.

FREEZING DUTY
A winter encampment had to be guarded at all times, so sentries like this shivering soldier wrapped themselves in whatever they could find to keep off the cold. This man has bundled himself in a blanket coat and wrapped his head and feet in cloth rags.

Leather strap

ICE CREEPERS
Bound with leather straps to shoes or boots, these iron cleats allowed a soldier to cross a frozen surface without slipping. Men in winter camp worked outside caring for livestock, erecting buildings, and fetching water and firewood.

VISITING THE TROOPS
General Washington, left, rides out from headquarters to see how well his men are keeping warm and dry. Accompanied by French volunteer the Marquis de Lafayette, Washington makes sure the sentries are alert and on guard, like the soldier standing at attention before him.

WASHINGTON'S LIFE GUARD
On duty at a winter encampment, this dashing soldier is a member of the corps that protected General Washington. Called the "Life Guard," this unit of specially chosen men numbered between 180–250 during the war. The men of the Life Guard protected headquarters and lived near the general's residence.

Officer's uniform

THE SOLDIER'S WINTER HOME
Close quarters, but warm, a log hut held twelve men, who slept on bunks three high. Loose straw covered with a blanket served as bedding, and it was in his bunk that the soldier kept his few personal effects—clothing, letters, Bible, and playing cards.

OFFICER'S TRUNK
The few possessions an American officer brought with him to camp could be carried in this leather-covered trunk. The inside is lined with blue paper, the outside studded with brass tacks that protect it during rough handling.

MOUTH HARP
This musical instrument gave a twanging sound when it was held between the teeth and the steel vibrator, which is missing in the picture, was plucked.

Iron mouth harp

Missing steel vibrator would be here

BUILDING LOG HUTS IN THE SNOW
It was already cold and snow had fallen by the time the American army withdrew from the field after a warm-weather campaign. Before troops could go into winter encampment, they had to build their own shelters, hundreds of them. Men chopped down logs in the forest and carried them to huts under construction, while teams of oxen hauled heavier loads and flattened roadways through deep snow.

Symbols of freedom

THE EARLY FLAG OF THE UNITED STATES HAD 13 STRIPES TO represent the states, and it displayed the Union Jack to honor the colonies' British heritage. When independence became the goal, Congress adopted a new flag with a field of stars for the states. Philadelphia's "Liberty Bell," which rang out to celebrate the Declaration of Independence, became a symbol of the Revolution. So did artifacts once used on the battlefield or owned by patriots. Another celebration of liberty was "Yankee Doodle," a well-known tune sung by Redcoats with verses mocking Americans. New verses soon were composed by patriots, who expressed the pride of the revolutionaries: "Yankee Doodle is the tune / That we all delight in; / It suits for feasts, it suits for fun, / And just as well for fighting!" One revolutionary symbol, the "Liberty Cap," became a popular element on weather vanes for many years to come.

THE NATIONAL COLORS
The first American flag was the "Grand Union" flag, combining the British Union Jack and 13 stripes for each state. On June 14, 1777, Congress resolved the flag of the United States would be 13 stars on a blue field and 13 red and white stripes. No definite arrangement of the stars was determined, so various designs were used at first: one had stars in a circle, others had the stars arranged as seen above.

THE BETSY ROSS TALE
In 1777, the new United States needed a "national color" to replace the "Grand Union" flag that bore the British Union Jack. Once the new design of stars and stripes was approved by Congress, legend has it, Philadelphia seamstress Elizabeth "Betsy" Ross was asked by General Washington to sew the first national flag. No historical evidence other than a Ross family tradition backs up the Betsy Ross legend, yet it has been popularized in histories and celebrated in many dramatic illustrations.

LIBERTY BELL
In 1751, Pennsylvania ordered a bell from England for the new state house. Inscribed "Proclaim Liberty thro' all the land," the bell cracked the first time it was rung and had to be repaired. In use for more than 75 years, it tolled sadly in 1765, when the hated Stamp Act went into effect, and joyously to celebrate the act's repeal. In 1776, it rang even more joyously for the Declaration of Independence. It cracked again in 1835.

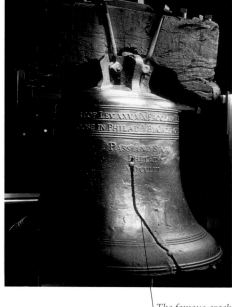

The famous crack

NG OF DEFIANCE
rly in the Revolution, the song ankee Doodle" was sung by dcoats whose verses mocked w England "Yankee" militiamen, ling them "doodles," or fools. ter, when the Yankees were torious in battle, they hurled the ult back at the British by singing "Yankee Doodle" melody with w, patriotic words.

Ropes for tension

Leather lugs for tightening ropes

Hoops

Drum body, painted

Militia fife

FIFE AND DRUM OF FREEDOM
This applewood military fife was played by Jonathan Curtis of Concord, Massachusetts, a militiaman in the Revolution. The drum belonged to militiaman William Diamond of Lexington, Massachusetts, who beat out the signal for his companions to muster and confront the Redcoats on Lexington Common on April 19, 1775, where the first shots of the war were fired.

Liberty cap design

Painted finish

Walking stick made from crab tree wood

Tassel

LIBERTY CAP IN IRON
One of the symbols of the American Revolution was a knitted hat with a dangling tassel. Known as a "Liberty Cap," it was worn defiantly as a statement of a radical political position. The cap was so popular that iron weather vanes were forged into the cap's shape, painted, and fixed proudly to the peaks and cupolas of barns and houses.

FRANKLIN'S GIFT TO WASHINGTON
Benjamin Franklin specified in his will that his "fine crab tree walking stick with a gold head curiously wrought in the form of a cap of liberty" would be left to his "friend and the friend of mankind, General Washington." Franklin died in 1790.

France becomes an ally

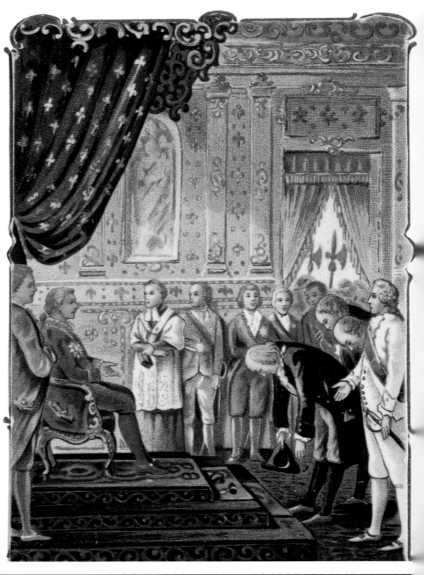

AMERICA DESPERATELY NEEDED MILITARY SUPPLIES, cash, and a navy. That meant finding allies. The most obvious was France, eager to avenge defeat by Britain in the Seven Years' War. By mid-1776, France was secretly sending financial aid and supplies to support the Revolution, but more was needed. That year, Benjamin Franklin traveled to Paris to arrange a formal alliance with King Louis XVI. Much admired in France as a diplomat, inventor, and writer, Franklin was head of the American negotiators, who included John Adams. The Americans found a friend in the foreign minister Comte de (Count of) Vergennes, who masterminded France's war efforts. More cash—gifts and loans—went to America, as did shiploads of military supplies. By early 1778, a state of war existed between France and Britain. Adventurous French officers volunteered for the American army, one of the best being the Marquis de Lafayette. Eventually, more than 12,000 French troops would fight in America under their main commander, Comte de Rochambeau.

A NOBLE VOLUNTEER
In 1777, French nobleman Marquis de Lafayette volunteered as an aide to General Washington. Unlike some French officers, who demanded a high rank, Lafayette modestly offered to do whatever was needed. An excellent officer, he quickly became a general.

Crown

GOLDEN LOUIS
This French Louis D'Or gold piece was a boon to the Revolution when it, and thousands more just like it, arrived in America as a gift from France. Decorated with the fleur-de-lis and the likeness of the French king, the "Louis" helped turn the tide in favor of the Revolution.

Image of King Louis XVI

Fleur-de-lis

FRENCH ROYAL SYMBOL
The fleur-de-lis, or "lily flower," decorated the coat of arms of the Bourbons, the French royal house.

FRANKLIN AT THE FRENCH COURT
Scientist, inventor, philosopher, writer, and diplomat Benjamin Franklin was famous throughout France and warmly welcomed when he and the American delegation arrived in 1777. They were presented at the royal palace of Versailles to King Louis XVI, who approved financial and military support crucial to the success of the Revolution.

JOHN ADAMS INSPECTS FRENCH MARINES

The French army included several regiments of Irish-born troops, who often wore red uniforms. These men, who are being inspected by American diplomat John Adams in l'Orient on the coast of France, are Irishmen from the Regiment de Walsh-Serrant. They have volunteered as marines for the American warship *Bonhomme Richard*. The ship was commanded by John Paul Jones, who made raids from French ports.

FRENCH SWORD

There were many types and sizes of swords, from the cavalryman's heavy saber to this light and slender French "small sword," ideal for an infantry officer. The blade is iron, with silver decorating the hilt—as the handle was called.

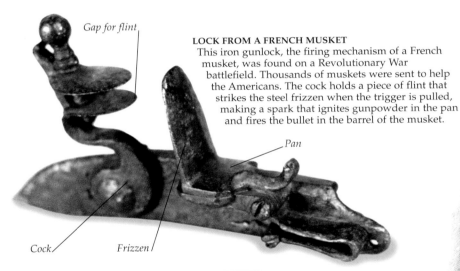

LOCK FROM A FRENCH MUSKET

This iron gunlock, the firing mechanism of a French musket, was found on a Revolutionary War battlefield. Thousands of muskets were sent to help the Americans. The cock holds a piece of flint that strikes the steel frizzen when the trigger is pulled, making a spark that ignites gunpowder in the pan and fires the bullet in the barrel of the musket.

Gap for flint

Pan

Cock

Frizzen

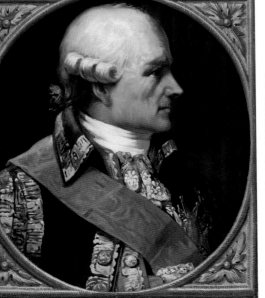

THE FRENCH COMMANDER

The leader of French troops in North America, Jean Baptiste Donatien de Vimeur, Comte de Rochambeau, had high regard for George Washington. Rochambeau commanded more than 7,000 well-equipped French soldiers. He treated Washington and the Americans as equals, even though the Revolutionary army was weak and impoverished compared to the French. At one point, Rochambeau opened his army's war chest to Washington, offering to share half of the money it held.

COMTE DE VERGENNES

French foreign minister Charles Gravier, Comte de Vergennes, was a key player in the early secret contributions of funds and supplies to the American revolutionaries. Vergennes aimed to weaken the British Empire so France could become the world's greatest power. France's support of America led to all-out war in 1778.

The war at sea

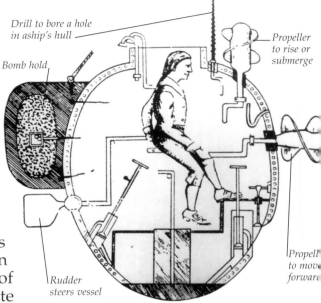

Drill to bore a hole in aship's hull

Bomb hold

Propeller to rise or submerge

Rudder steers vessel

Propell to move forware

AMERICANS LACKED WARSHIPS to challenge the powerful British Navy, but soon tried a new invention: the submarine. In 1776, the *Turtle* attempted to attach a bomb beneath a warship in New York harbor. When the plan failed, submarines were forgotten for decades to come. British ships dominated American waters until the French fleet arrived to challenge them in 1778. The French were unsuccessful in the beginning, mainly because the first French admiral to appear, Comte d'Estaing, was inexperienced. While huge sea battles raged between French and British fleets in Caribbean and European waters, the Americans had triumphs of their own. Congress authorized private ship owners—"privateers,"—to attack enemy vessels. Military stores brought back by privateers and by merchant ships that ran the British blockade were essential to the Revolutionary cause. John Paul Jones was the best of the American commanders.

THE *TURTLE*
The first combat submarine, called the *Turtle*, went into action in September 1776 in New York harbor. Its one-man crew tried unsuccessfully to attach a bomb to the hull of a British warship.

A FRENCH ADMIRAL
Admiral Charles Comte d'Estaing was an unsuccessful French leader. In 1778, he failed to seal off, "blockade," New York harbor. Next, he refused to aid an American attack on Rhode Island, and later could not wipe out weaker enemy squadrons in the Caribbean. He was wounded in a defeat at Savannah in 1779.

NAVAL FLAGS
The British Royal Navy's flag, or ensign, has the Union Jack in the upper left corner, on a red field. The independent states designed flags for their own warships. South Carolina's ships displayed a rattlesnake with the warning, "Don't tread on me."

Royal Navy ensign

South Carolina naval flag

SEAMEN WANTED!
Posters called for sailors to enlist with commander John Paul Jones and make their fortunes. When an enemy vessel was captured— made a "prize"—it was sold off and the money divided among the victorious officers and crew.

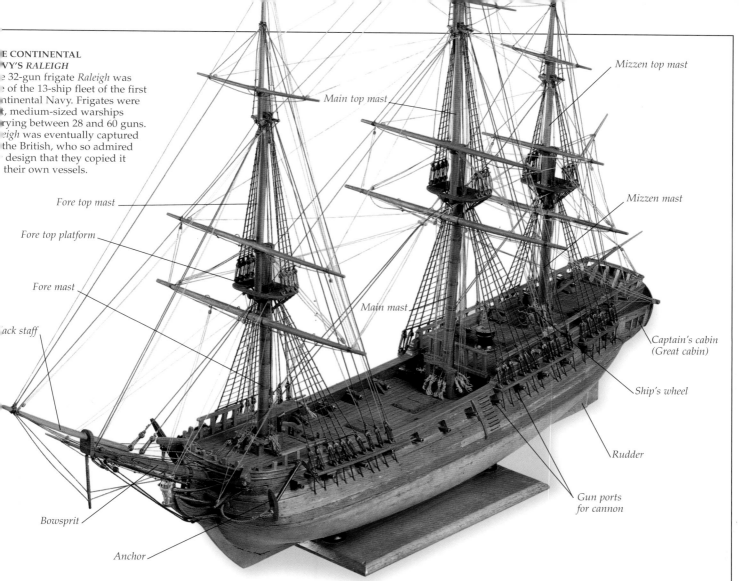

e 32-gun frigate *Raleigh* was
e of the 13-ship fleet of the first
ntinental Navy. Frigates were
t, medium-sized warships
rying between 28 and 60 guns.
eigh was eventually captured
the British, who so admired
design that they copied it
their own vessels.

Mizzen top mast

Main top mast

Mizzen mast

Fore top mast

Fore top platform

Main mast

Fore mast

Captain's cabin
(Great cabin)

ack staff

Ship's wheel

Rudder

Bowsprit

Gun ports
for cannon

Anchor

battle to the death

n Paul Jones captured many British merchant
sels and also won victories against warships.
1779, Jones led his *Bonhomme Richard* in a fatal
tle with the enemy's flagship, *Serapis*—
sspelled "*Seraphis*" in the art at right. The
tish captain saw the American ship was sinking
d demanded Jones's surrender. Jones answered,
nave not yet begun to fight!" He captured the
apis as his own vessel went down. In 1787, a
teful Congress honored Jones with a gold
dal for his service.

Revolutionary
warship

John Paul
Jones

'87 John Paul Jones Medal

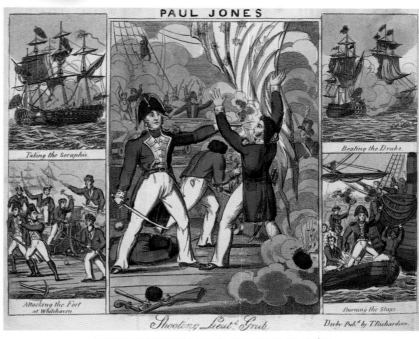

PAUL JONES

Taking the Seraphis.

Beating the Drake.

Attacking the Fort
at Whitehaven

Shooting Lieut.ᵗ Grub.

Burning the Ships

Derby Pub.ᵈ by T.Richardson.

SCENES FROM THE CAREER OF JOHN PAUL JONES
John Paul Jones was a daring commander of a Continental Navy squadron. The central
image shows Jones attacking one of his officers, who wanted to surrender during battle
with the *Serapis*. Jones eventually seized the enemy ship—picture top right.

Embattled New York

IN 1775, PATROIT ACTIVISTS SUCH AS Alexander Hamilton and the Sons of Liberty were outnumbered by Loyalists in New York City, which was bitterly divided. After losing Boston early in 1776, Sir William Howe captured New York that summer, driving out Washington and the rebel sympathizers. Patriots burned down part of New York, but Redcoats held on to the city for the rest of the war. Loyalists fled there by the thousands, causing overcrowding and food shortages. Folk in the besieged city tried to go on with their lives, holding theatrical performances and bright social events. Yet, the many burned houses still lay in ruins, and troops had to be quartered in churches and public buildings. After peace was made, the last British soldiers left New York on November 25, 1783. This was known as "Evacuation Day," and Washington and his few remaining officers rode in to take back the city.

BATTLE FOR A LIBERTY POLE
Before the Revolution, Patriots and Redcoats sometimes clashed in New York City. Often, Liberty Poles were the cause of hostility. Symbols of resistance to the British, Liberty Poles were raised by Patriots and torn down by soldiers after bloody fights.

THE BEGGAR'S OPERA
New York was known for its lively theaters, and the most popular musical play of the period was "The Beggar's Opera." A comedy that made fun of high society, "The Beggar's Opera" was enjoyed by citizens, as well as Redcoat officers and soldiers.

ALEXANDER HAMILTON
(1755–1804)
Born in the West Indies, Hamilton came to New York while in his teens. He studied at King's College and became an active Patriot, serving as an artilleryman. Hamilton later became Washington's military secretary and was known as the "Pen of the Army."

SIR HENRY CLINTON (1738–95)
Known for bravery on the battlefield, Clinton was Howe's top lieutenant general during the invasion of New York in 1776. In 1778, he succeeded Howe in overall command, but resigned in 1781 after failing to achieve victory over the revolutionaries.

DOWNING THE KING'S STATUE
A celebration was held in July 1776, when the Declaration of Independence was read to the American army occupying New York. Wanting more excitement, a mob at the Bowling Green tore down a lead statue of King George and chopped off its head.

GERMAN TROOPS LAND IN NEW YORK
The British hired regiments of German soldiers to fight in America. Germans helped capture New York in 1776, then occupied Manhattan.

he great fire

the British moved into New York in 1776,
shington wanted to prevent use of the city as
British base. Although it is not known if direct
ers were given, rebel infiltrators soon set
ch of New York ablaze, destroying
ildings that would have become
dcoat barracks and residences.

BURNING AND KILLING
As buildings in New York roared into flame on September 21, 1776, British
soldiers beat and bayonetted suspected arsonists. Servants salvaged what they
could from the fires, but the destruction was widespread. For years to come, the
lack of housing was a hardship for occupying soldier and civilian alike.

int

TINDER LIGHTER
Like a flintlock musket, this lighter
sparked to ignite tinder—
flammable material kept dry
in a box. Burning tinder
would then be used to
ignite kindling to start a
fire. A steel striker was
struck against flint to
create a spark.

Tinder box

Steel striker

FLYING THE STARS
AND STRIPES
British soldiers leaving New
York nailed the Union Jack
to a flagpole, making it
difficult to get down. While
Redcoats watched, a Patriot
climbed up, tore off the
flag, and put up the Stars
and Stripes instead.

TRIUMPHANT ENTRY INTO THE CITY
Washington's main army had been disbanded by November 25, 1783,   York City from the departing British. Known as "Evacuation Day," this
when he and a small group of officers rode in to take possession of New   date was celebrated in New York for many years to come.

Spies and traitors

DURING THE REVOLUTION, SECRET MESSAGES were sometimes written in code, often hidden in shoe heels, and at least once in a hollow silver bullet. If disguised couriers and spies were captured, they were hanged. This was the fate of Nathan Hale, a 20-year-old Continental officer caught while spying in New York in 1776. One patriot courier was Deborah Champion, who rode more than 75 miles from her home in Connecticut, carrying military dispatches to George Washington near Boston. She was allowed to pass by British patrols who considered her harmless. Through much of the war, Washington counted on Major Benjamin Tallmadge to meet secretly with undercover agents and to keep them provided with money. New Jersey-born Patience Wright, who lived in England during the war, hid messages inside sculptures that she made and shipped back to American patriots. The most notorious traitor was Benedict Arnold, a rebel general who turned against the Revolution. Arnold's plan to surrender West Point in 1780 was uncovered in the nick of time.

A PATRIOT WOMAN'S CLOAK
During Washington's 1775–76 siege of Boston, Deborah Champion (1753–1845) secretly carried messages and the army payroll to rebel troops there. Wearing this hooded cloak, Champion rode from Norwich, Connecticut, with dispatches and funds sent by her father, General Henry Champion.

WASHINGTON'S SPYMASTER
Dragoon major Benjamin Tallmadge (1754–1835) was a link between Washington and secret agents operating in and around British-controlled New York City. Quick action by Tallmadge in 1780 revealed that captured Major John André was a British spy, exposing Benedict Arnold's plot to betray West Point, a key fort on the Hudson River.

COIN FOR CONSPIRACIES
Very little "hard money," as coins were termed, existed in Revolutionary America, and what there was included Spanish silver reales, sometimes cut into several pieces. Spies had to be paid, and secret messengers needed cash to buy horses or pay for ferries or food, and any silver money would do.

Silver coin cut into quarter

A LIFE FOR THE CAUSE OF LIBERTY
In mid-1776, Connecticut Patriot officer Nathan Hale slipped into occupied New York City disguised as a schoolmaster. While observing British defenses, he was taken prisoner and sentenced to be hanged. Legend has it that Hale announced, "I regret that I have but one life to give for my country!"

HOLLOW BULLET
A piece of paper bearing a message from one British commander to another was folded tightly and concealed in this hollow bullet made of silver.

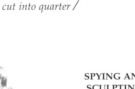

SPYING AND SCULPTING
Famous for fashioning heads out of putty or wax, American-born sculptor Patience Wright owned a studio in London. A supporter of the rebel cause, Wright conversed with her subjects about British military plans, then passed on to Patriot agents whatever she learned.

CAPTURED AND EXPOSED

Traveling in disguise after secretly meeting American turncoat Benedict Arnold in 1780, British major John André was stopped by rebel sentries, who discovered a suspicious message hidden in the heel of his boot. André was condemned and hanged as a spy. Many on both sides, including Washington, regretted the execution of so fine an officer.

Turncoat hero

General Benedict Arnold had great success on the battlefield, but he came to despise Congress when it placed other officers ahead of him in rank. Disillusioned with the Revolution, he conspired in 1780 to help the British capture West Point. When the plot was discovered, he escaped to join the British. The royal army had little use for his services, however, so Arnold went to England with his wife and children.

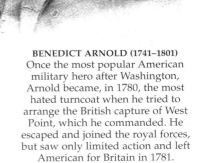

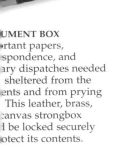

...UMENT BOX

...rtant papers, ...spondence, and ...ary dispatches needed ... sheltered from the ...ents and from prying ... This leather, brass, ...canvas strongbox ...d be locked securely ...otect its contents.

A LOYAL WIFE

Philadelphian Peggy (Shippen) Arnold married Benedict Arnold when he was commander of that city's Patriot garrison. She was with him during the West Point espionage affair but was not considered a co-conspirator. Afterward, she and their son, Edward, were allowed to rejoin Arnold behind British lines.

BENEDICT ARNOLD (1741–1801)

Once the most popular American military hero after Washington, Arnold became, in 1780, the most hated turncoat when he tried to arrange the British capture of West Point, which he commanded. He escaped and joined the royal forces, but saw only limited action and left American for Britain in 1781.

Home front and behind the lines

THE REVOLUTION WAS A BITTER CIVIL WAR, with Americans divided into three equal camps: Patriots, Loyalists, and neutrals. The armies in the field were small, only a few thousand on each side, but for eight long years a vast country from Maine to Georgia was in a state of war. Loyalists gathered in cities that were British strongholds, while Patriots gained military control of most of the countryside. People changed sides according to which army was in power locally, and those who wanted to remain neutral were often harassed by both armies. In country between the hostile forces, such as New Jersey and southern New York, no one was safe from raiders and pillagers, both military and civilian. Yet, life went on according to the seasons, and families worked hard to survive, hoping war would not sweep their way. Most Americans made the best of things, stayed warm by their own firesides, met neighbors at the public house, and kept out of the fighting.

AFTER PLANTING, THE HOEING
To keep weeds down between the rows of corn, vegetables, and tobacco, farmers worked the earth with an iron hoe attached to a stout handle.

FARM WORK GOES ON
Most Americans lived on family farms during the Revolution, and despite the war, planting and harvesting had to be done according to the seasons. The crops depended on the simple plow, held by the strong-backed farmer while draft animals pulled.

REDCOAT PILLAGING
Although British and American soldiers were not encouraged to raid farmsteads and steal from houses, it often happened that civilians known to support one cause were treated severely by hostile soldiers. These Redcoats, with officers and the distraught family looking on, are ransacking a house in New Jersey. A male member of the family has been injured and lies stunned nearby.

he public house

~~verns~~ and inns were known as "public houses,"
~~w~~ere folk gathered to drink and eat, read newspapers,
~~sh~~are stories, and gossip—as well as gamble at dice and cards.
~~Al~~so called "ordinaries," the public house offered room and board
~~to~~ travelers. Political meetings were often held in public houses,
~~as~~ neighbors debated the important issues of the day.

A FAVORITE PIPE
In public houses, clay pipes were available
to guests. A small piece of the end was
broken off so the guest would have
a fresh stem to smoke.

HUNGRY FOR NEWS
~~P~~atrons of a New York City coffeehouse read the newspapers, which might
~~c~~onsist of recent editions published in the British-occupied city, month-old
~~pa~~pers from England, or journals from rebel-held New Jersey. As many as 40
~~ne~~wspapers thrived in the colonies in Revolutionary times, publishing news,
announcements, and advertisements.

Wooden
staves

Green-lead glass bottle

Fill hole

Corkscrew

Iron hoops bind
wooden staves

A KEG FOR STRONG DRINK
Brewed and distilled spirits
were consumed widely in
America, where water was
often too polluted to drink.
Instead, hard cider and beer
quenched the thirst. The most
common alcoholic beverage
was rum, stored in wooden
kegs sealed by a cork.

Hearth and home

Home life centered on the hearth, where food
was cooked and hands warmed. The hearth
might be made of brick, cut stone, or dried
clay, but it always had to have a ready
supply of kindling and firewood—the task
of the children, who fetched it from the
woodshed. Family, servants, and farmhands
came together in the kitchen-gathering room
beside the fire burning in the hearth.

~~ed~~ bodice

Brown tabby
silk material

A PRIZED JUG
Pottery works were found
throughout America, but
family heirlooms brought
from Europe were treasured
and handed down through
the generations. This Rhenish
jug is gray salt-glazed
stoneware, probably brought
over from Germany.

COMFORTABLE AND GRACIOUS
The woman's everyday dress of
the period combined grace and
elegance with practicality and
comfort. The close-fitting bodice
~~a~~bove a petticoat and full overskirt
allowed freedom of movement
while modestly concealing the
woman's ankles from view.

Finely dressed
colonial doll

THE FAMILY MEAL
The women of the house were in charge of the kitchen and the hearth, and
spent many hours preparing food, preserving fruits and vegetables, drying
herbs, and smoking meat. The hearth was almost always in use, although in
warm climates families often used outside kitchens, too.

Camps and prisons

FEEDING AND EQUIPPING THE ARMIES came before caring for captured enemy soldiers, so prisoners from both sides were poorly treated. Always short of money, both Congress and Parliament tried to avoid war expenses as much as they could. This meant ignoring the needs of prisoners, who were too often treated inhumanely. British prison ships were notoriously cruel, and so were Patriot prison camps where captured Loyalists and Redcoats were kept. Wealthy prisoners, such as Patriot diplomat Henry Laurens, could purchase what they needed to survive, but most captured soldiers were in for a desperate experience. It was no wonder that prisoners were badly cared for since the enlisted soldier also was often neglected. While British soldiers were far better fed and equipped than Americans, both depended on their camp followers to give them comfort. The women and merchants following the armies provided food, drink, and welcome companionship to the off-duty soldier.

IMPRISONED IN THE TOWER
A former president of Congress, South Carolina patriot Henry Laurens (1724–92) was captured while journeying by ship in 1780. Laurens was thrown into the infamous Tower of London and threatened with execution. Exchanged for General Cornwallis, Laurens went to Paris as a peace delegate.

Door for replacing extinguished candle

CANDLE LANTERN
Iron lanterns with candles inside were carried around or suspended on a hook. These lanterns gave little light, but few people went out after dark, especially since candles were scarce in wartime.

WORTHLESS MONEY
Congress created its own "Continental" money, coins and paper dollars to be spent for the war effort. Many people did not want to accept Continental money in payment, however, because the rebels might lose the war, which would make the money worthless.

UNLOADING ESSENTIAL SUPPLIES
Military encampments required a steady flow of loaded wagons to feed, clothe, shelter, and equip the troops. Rugged Conestoga covered wagons pulled by teams of four to six oxen or horses were capable of hauling 15,000 pounds of cargo over rough roads. During the first years of the war, Patriot encampments received little in the way of supplies or equipment and men made do with half rations.

The fortunes of war

Prisons for the enlisted men of both sides were unhealthy, cruel places, where thousands died or permanently lost their health because of the abuse of their captors. Officers were treated far better, and were usually exchanged for an enemy prisoner of equal rank. The average soldier, however, was thrown into a hell-hole of captivity and left to rot for years, with a slim chance for survival or recovery.

CAVERNS CALLED "HELL"
Just as cruel as British prison ships, the American prison in the copper mines of Newgate, Connecticut, took the lives or health of many hundred captured Loyalists. Prisoners were forced to work deep beneath the surface in caverns they called "Hell." These men were brutally treated by their guards, who despised them for opposing the Revolution.

THE CRUEL PRISON SHIPS
Patriot prisoners in the New York area were crammed into old ships anchored around the city. These "prison hulks," such as the *Jersey*, anchored off Brooklyn, were damp, filthy, and cold, causing hundreds of starved prisoners to fall ill and die. Vicious military guards added to the woes of those Americans unfortunate enough to be kept in the prison hulks.

Following the troops

For every army in the field or in camp, there were crowds of civilians who stayed close by. These "camp followers" included wives and children of soldiers and merchants who sold wares to the troops. When not marching or fighting, soldiers had considerable freedom to visit their families among the camp followers, enjoying meals that were better than army fare.

Spoon carved from deer antler

EATING UTENSILS
With long hours in camp, soldiers had time to carve bone and horn and whittle wood. Among their creations were spoons and cups, which were needed to replace utensils lost while campaigning. A fine fork was precious— hard to come by for a soldier with no money in an army that was just as poor.

Brass fork with wooden handle

Carved initials, "WCW"

Drinking cup made from a horn

Legs to stand over flame

Gridiron for cooking over campfire

COOKING FOR THE TROOPS
Camp followers were also found near prisoner-of-war enclosures, and a certain amount of communication was allowed between captives and their families. These folk cooked on open fires in their own encampments, often selling food to captive and sentry alike. Many women earned a little money by washing the laundry of men from both armies.

The soldier's doctor

In 1775, the colonies had about 3,500 physicians, but only 400 had university degrees. The rest had learned their skills through apprenticeship. Few trained doctors served with the Revolutionary armies. One leading Patriot physician, Dr. Benjamin Rush of Philadelphia, wrote a manual on keeping soldiers healthy, but diseases such as smallpox, typhus, and malaria killed ten times more men than died in battle. Because Congress did not provide the needed funds, military hospitals were short-staffed and lacked supplies, medicine, and healthful food. Medicines of the day ranged from herbal remedies to prepared mixtures of powdered drugs and chemicals, but little was available to military hospitals. There, conditions were primitive: surgical tools for extracting bullets, amputating limbs, and drawing blood were not sterilized or even washed, and bandages were reused. Many men died from minor wounds that became infected and did not heal. In time, better hospitals were designed, improving chances for recovery.

BENJAMIN RUSH
A leading patriot and politician, Dr. Benjamin Rush served as a Continental Army medical administrator, but resigned in frustration over the hospital department's incompetence. Rush went on to be an influential American physician, writer, and educator.

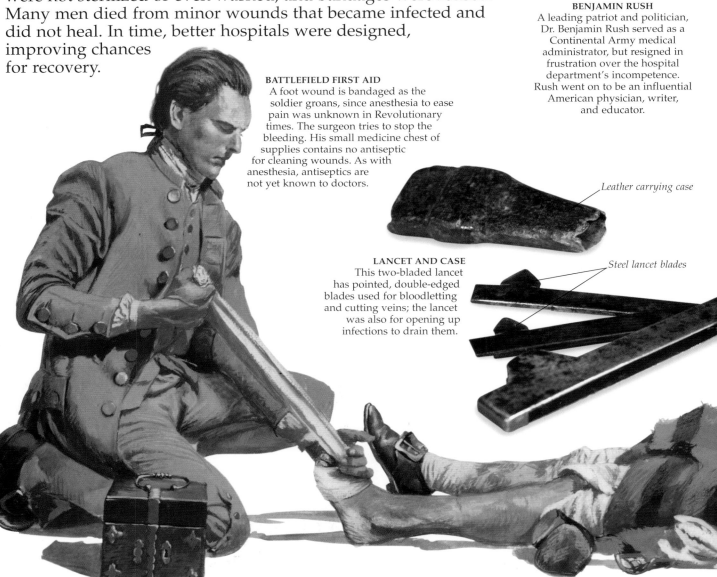

BATTLEFIELD FIRST AID
A foot wound is bandaged as the soldier groans, since anesthesia to ease pain was unknown in Revolutionary times. The surgeon tries to stop the bleeding. His small medicine chest of supplies contains no antiseptic for cleaning wounds. As with anesthesia, antiseptics are not yet known to doctors.

Leather carrying case

LANCET AND CASE
This two-bladed lancet has pointed, double-edged blades used for bloodletting and cutting veins; the lancet was also for opening up infections to drain them.

Steel lancet blades

IMPROVED HOSPITALS

Military planners eventually built specially designed cabins to replace crowded, unhealthy sick chambers in tents and private homes. This Valley Forge hospital hut was built to allow the free flow of air, which helped improve patients' health.

THE APOTHECARY'S ART

Apothecaries made, mixed, and sold drugs, but most families used homegrown medicinal herbs. For serious illnesses the apothecary had imported drugs—such as cinchona bark for malaria—and prepared purgatives to cleanse the system: ipecac, tartar emetic, and jalap.

Side compartments swing open on hinges, showing more storage space

Compartments for storing medicines

PORTABLE MEDICINE CHEST

Military physicians kept medicines in a wooden chest that also held syringes, sponges, forceps, bandages, twine, and pharmaceutical equipment for weighing and mixing ingredients. Hospitals used large chests, with 80 or more different medicines, while regimental surgeons in the field carried smaller chests.

Cupping glass

Medicine bottle

Medical equipment

Old bandages were pulled apart by iron forceps to see if the wound was healing. Placing a glass cup against the skin—"cupping"—drew blood and pus to the surface. A pewter bowl caught blood and fluids but was seldom used for water because wounds were not cleaned.

Pewter bowl

Cupping glass

Forceps

War for the South

Late in 1778, the war shifted to the South as the British captured Savannah, Georgia. In October 1779, they defeated a force of Americans and French who tried to lay siege to Savannah. In the spring of 1780, Charleston, South Carolina, fell to royal forces, and General Charles Cornwallis took command of the king's army. Cornwallis soon destroyed an American force at Camden, South Carolina. His triumphant officers included cavalryman Banastre Tarleton, notorious for slaughtering captured rebels. George Washington sent Nathanael Greene of Rhode Island to take charge in the South. Although Greene lost several battles, he inflicted heavy British casualties that seriously weakened Cornwallis. Other American commanders won important victories—at King's Mountain, North Carolina, October 1780, and Cowpens, South Carolina, January 1781. In March, Cornwallis defeated Greene at Guilford Court House, North Carolina, but suffered great losses. Cornwallis withdrew to the sea, and eventually to Yorktown, Virginia, to await support that would never come.

DEATH OF PULASKI
Polish volunteer, General Casimir Pulaski, was killed leading a charge at the 1779 Siege of Savannah, a defeat for an army of Americans and French. Pulaski had served in the American army since 1777. He performed gallantly in many battles, including Germantown and Brandywine.

Iron blade, 35 inches long

Hilt

HORSEMAN'S SABER
This heavy, curved sword, called a saber, belonged to an American cavalryman. A trooper learned to use the saber while also managing a horse—practicing slashes and thrusts and blocking opponents' blades.

A DANGEROUS ENEMY
British dragoon commander Lieutenant Colonel Banastre Tarleton was hated by Americans, who named him "Butcher" for his ruthless policy of taking no prisoners. Tarleton served throughout the war and was most successful when leading hard-hitting Loyalist troopers on sudden raids.

Bright red fabric cut from the back of a chair

DRAGOON FLAG
Cut from fabric that covered the back of a chair, this flag was carried into the Battle of Cowpens by William Washington's dragoons, who followed it to a smashing victory.

The Roman numeral "VII" shows this is the flag of the 7th Fusiliers

CAPTURED COLORS
At Cowpens, Morgan's troops captured the regimental flag of the British 7th Fusiliers, proud Redcoat professionals. Tarleton lost more than 320 dead and wounded, and 600 others were taken prisoner. American casualties were 22 killed, 60 wounded.

Regimental bad

BATTLES IN THE SOUTH
The British won most battles in the South—including Savannah, Charleston, Camden, and Guilford Court House. Yet, the region was too large to capture and hold; American commander Nathanael Greene organized fresh resistance wherever the enemy marched.

CAVALRY FIGHT AT COWPENS, SOUTH CAROLINA

Servant rescuing William Washington

h dragoons of Tarleton's Legion surround American cavalry commander lonel William Washington, at the Battle of Cowpens. Washington, on the ite horse, was in mortal danger until his body servant, left, fired a pistol, wounding an attacker. Another American dragoon arrived to drive the enemy away. Tarleton's 1,100-man British and Loyalist army was wiped out by an American force of about the same size under General Daniel Morgan.

he key to final victory

athanael Greene was perhaps Washington's best general. eene served in the field and at one point also took arge of military supply. In the South, his strategy was to ep the men fighting and avoid crushing defeats. He was rsued for months by the main British army, while other bel commanders attacked enemy supply lines and forts. late 1781, almost all British posts outside Charleston d Savannah were abandoned.

LOST THE BATTLES, BUT WON THE SOUTH
Rhode Islander Nathanael Greene commanded rebel forces in the South. He inflicted heavy losses on Cornwallis, who withdrew to Yorktown in 1781, hoping for reinforcements.

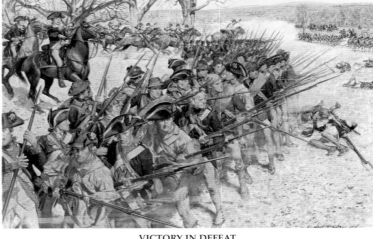

VICTORY IN DEFEAT
In 1781, Greene's force of 4,400 Continentals and militia took on the advancing Cornwallis at Guilford Court House, North Carolina. The British had only 1,900 men, but most were seasoned regulars. The battle was bitter, with furious hand-to-hand fighting. Cornwallis held the field but suffered more than 500 casualties. Greene lost fewer—78 were killed and 183 wounded.

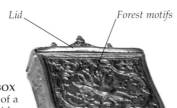

Lid   *Forest motifs*

CARTRIDGE BOX
Probably once the property of a German soldier, this brass cartridge box kept ammunition safe and dry. Cartridges were made of paper wrapped around a measured amount of black powder and a lead ball.

SHOT BAGS
Revolutionary militia soldiers sometimes carried hunting firearms into battle; these leather shot bags held five bird-shot balls, which were smaller than the musket or rifle balls of military firearms.

Plug top

Yorktown

DURING 1781, GENERAL CORNWALLIS almost wiped out Patriot armed resistance in the South but could not destroy the elusive Nathanael Greene, who skillfully held his fighting force together. By August, Cornwallis and his 7,500 veterans were at Yorktown, Virginia, awaiting reinforcements and supplies from British-held New York. Washington and French general De Rochambeau swiftly moved to trap Cornwallis, and the French fleet arrived to blockade Yorktown. The Franco-American armies numbered more than 17,000 troops. When the British fleet appeared in September, French admiral De Grasse drove it back to New York, maintaining the blockade. Avoiding costly frontal attacks, Washington fired devastating artillery barrages day after day, until Cornwallis gave up. On October 19, the defeated royal army marched out of Yorktown to yield their muskets and proud flags to the victors. Washington, however, would be cheated of his greatest triumph, for Cornwallis said he was ill and sent his second-in-command to surrender the army. Yorktown was the last major battle of the Revolution.

WASHINGTON AT YORKTOWN
Riding alongside the Marquis de Lafayette, his dependable young general, George Washington directs American and French troops in this folk art painting of the great victory at Yorktown the fall of 1781. This was the final major battle of the Revolution

POCKET TELESCOPE
Observing enemy troop movements by telescope was essential to military leaders. On ships, telescopes showed flag signals from friendly vessels, especially from a commander's ship.

Eyepiece

Lens

BRITISH ADMIRAL HOOD
Sir Samuel Hood (1724–1816) tried to prevent the French navy from blockading Cornwallis. The French fleet engaged the forces of Hood and Admiral Thomas Graves and forced them to withdraw, leaving Cornwallis trapped.

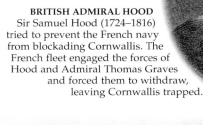

Screw cap protects lens

FRENCH ADMIRAL DE GRASSE
French warships under Admiral Francois de Grasse (1722–88) landed 3,000 soldiers to help besiege the British at Yorktown in September 1781. When enemy ships appeared, De Grasse fought them off after a two-hour battle, sealing Cornwallis's doom.

THE DECISIVE SEA BATTLE
De Grasse outfought British admirals Hood and Graves at the Battle of the Chesapeake Capes on September forcing them back to New York. If the British Navy had brought reinforcements or rescued Cornwallis, the Yorktown campaign would have been a failure and the war could have turned in favor of the British. This naval engagement was among the most important battles of the entire Revolution.

STORMING THE YORKTOWN REDOUBT

Washington moved his trenches and artillery steadily closer to the British fortifications by digging new works under cover of darkness. Cornwallis was forced into an ever-smaller defensive position. On October 14th, Captain Alexander Hamilton led a nighttime assault against a British redoubt, while French infantry attacked another. When the cannon captured in those redoubts were turned on Yorktown, Cornwallis had no choice but surrender.

THE DEADLY BAYONET
At the start of the Revolution, a bayonet wielded by a Redcoat was the most feared of weapons. By the end of the war, elite American troops also were skilled in bayonet attacks; this was how they captured a key strongpoint at Yorktown, forcing Cornwallis to give up.

ARTILLERYMAN'S LINSTOCK
Gunners at Yorktown used a linstock such as this to hold the smoldering match that fired a cannon. The match was brought to the touch hole, igniting the gunpowder that in turn fired the charge.

Spear point

Iron linstock piece is 14 inches long

Match rope

LORD CHARLES CORNWALLIS (1738–1805)
Cornwallis won battles but could not destroy the rebels. In mid-1781, he moved his army to Yorktown to wait for reinforcements that never came. After the war, he became governor general of India and a high official in the British government.

Wooden shaft

WASHINGTON'S GREATEST VICTORY
Cornwallis claimed to be too ill to attend the surrender ceremonies after Yorktown. Instead, the British second-in-command offered his sword to Washington, who refused it, directing the sword be given to his own second-in-command, General Benjamin Lincoln of Massachusetts.

The last two years of war

THE BATTLES ENDED WITH YORKTOWN, but the war would not be over until peace was signed. There were small clashes, and men still died. One of Washington's favorite aides was killed in a skirmish with Redcoats in South Carolina. Also, there were occasional enemy raids along the coast, which cost more lives. Washington promised to remain in the field until New York City, the last Redcoat foothold, was evacuated. Through much of 1782–83, Washington was with his army near Newburgh, New York. His officers and men were angry that Congress was unable to provide the back pay it owed them. In part to lift their spirits, the general created a special decoration, the "Badge of Military Merit." First awarded in 1783, it later became known as the "Purple Heart." In this time, Washington met with Sir Guy Carleton, the highly respected new British commander, to arrange the peaceful entry of American troops into New York on November 25, 1783.

LOSS OF LIFE CONTINUES
A former aide to Washington, and much admired for gallantry, Colonel John Laurens (c.1754–1782) was killed during a minor clash near Charleston in his native South Carolina. Laurens was the son of Henry Laurens, former president of Congress.

SEAL OF THE UNITED STATES
Congress agreed in 1782 on a final concept for America's official seal. Secretary of Congress Charles Thomson drew the above sketch, which was used as the basis for the seal design. The motto "E Pluribus Unum" means "One out of many."

Various caliber lead bullets

A CASUALTY'S HAT
Connecticut militiaman Phineas Meigs was 74 when he answered an alarm in 1782. A British warship was raiding East Guilford, and shots were exchanged. Meigs fell, mortally wounded in the head, the bullet passing through his hat. He was one of the last to die in the Revolution.

HEADQUARTERS ON THE HUDSON
Washington could have gone home to Mount Vernon during the winter of 1782–83, but he stayed with the army instead. He wanted to be with the troops to keep them well-disciplined until peace terms were finalized. The Americans were based near Newburgh, New York, about 50 miles North of British-held New York City. The general lived in the Hasbrouck house, with a long view southward down the Hudson River, where American tents can be seen.

The soldiers go home

Disbanding the Continental Army was done in stages during 1783, with several regiments at a time given leave. Once back home, the men were officially discharged, without getting the back pay owed them. Congress lacked the funds to pay the army. One reason the troops were discharged a few at a time was to avoid an angry mass mutiny by the unhappy men. Many returned home embittered that Congress had not kept its promises. Years would pass before the troops received their long-deserved pay and pensions.

FAREWELLS AT NEW WINDSOR
Revolutionary troops begin to leave their quarters at New Windsor, New York. The Hudson Highlands in the background were a strong position to prevent the British striking northward out of New York City. The New Windsor quarters were near enough to the enemy occupiers to threaten them with sudden attack.

A LOYALIST'S COAT
Munson Hoyt of Norwalk, Connecticut, owner of this coat, was a Loyalist lieutenant in the Prince of Wales Volunteer regiment. Hoyt relocated in New Brunswick, Canada, where thousands of Loyalists moved after being forced to flee their homes. He eventually returned to live in the United States.

SIR GUY CARLETON (1724–1808)
Carleton replaced Clinton as commander of British forces in America. Carleton worked closely with Washington to arrange a peaceful evacuation of Redcoats from New York in November 1783. Both commanders made sure there was no looting by mobs in the hours after the British left the city and before the American takeover.

THIRTEEN HEARTS, THIRTEEN VERSES
Celebrating American liberty, this printed linen handkerchief has 13 hearts for the new states and bears illustrations showing domestic scenes. Its 13 verses honor soldiers away at war and families working at home: "While they our Liberties defend/Let us to Husbandry attend."

Thirteen hearts

Domestic scenes

Stanzas of verse

The Purple Heart

To award soldiers for outstanding acts of courage, Washington created a "Badge of Military Merit" in the form of a purple cloth heart. The general wanted to show "The road to glory in a patriot army and a free country is thus open to all." Only three such badges were awarded—all in 1783. The badge was almost forgotten until 1932, the 200th anniversary of Washington's birth, when it was reactivated as the "Purple Heart," a decoration for individuals wounded in action.

esign of iginal rple heart

Modern-day purple heart

THE "BADGE OF MILITARY MERIT"
Washington awards "Purple Hearts" at his Newburgh, New York, headquarters in 1783. Sergeant William Brown of the 5th Connecticut Continental Line receives his badge while Sergeant Elijah Churchill of the 2nd Continental Light Dragoons awaits. Sergeant Daniel Bissell, Jr., of the 2nd Connecticut Regiment, was honored later.

Peace and the birth of a nation

LOCKET OF REMEMBRANCE
During the Revolution, patriot John Adams of Massachusetts was often away from his beloved wife, Abigail. When he went to Paris to negotiate the peace, he gave this locket to Abigail for her to remember him by.

F ROM MID-1782 UNTIL SEPTEMBER 1783, British and American delegates Paris negotiated peace terms. The Americans were led by Benjamin Fran and John Adams. The final 1783 Treaty of Paris recognized the independence of the United States, with the Mississippi River as its west boundary. A few weeks later, in December 1783, George Washington resigned as American commander in chief and returned to his beloved Mount Vernon. The end of the Revolutionary War did not, however, guarantee the states would unite under one government. Several years of labor, debate, and negotiations were required before a Constitution was drafted that all the states could accept. Important national leaders in this period included Robert Morris, who worked on plans to finance a federal government, and political thinker James Madison, who helped write the Constitution. The Constitution of the United States was drafted in 1787 and went into effect on March 4, 1789, as the fundamental law of the new nation.

PROVISIONAL PEACE AGREEMEN
The provisional, or preliminar peace treaty to end th Revolutionary War wa signed by the negotiato on November 30, 1782. required ten more months work out all the details of th final document, which wa approved on September 1783, and named th Treaty of Pari

AMERICAN PEACEMAKERS
Artist Benjamin West painted portraits of the American peace negotiators in Paris to include them in a larger painting along with British negotiators. Since the British refused to pose, West left them out of the picture. The Americans were, left to right, John Jay, John Adams, Benjamin Franklin, Henry Laurens, and William Temple Franklin, their secretary.

WASHINGTON SUBMITS HIS RESIGNATION
t the height of his glory as a conquering hero, George Washington faithfully returned
s commander in chief's commission to members of Congress assembled at Annapolis,
aryland, on December 23, 1783. King George, himself, was impressed that the widely
admired Washington resigned instead of choosing to become a military dictator.

The Society of the Cincinnati

GENERAL LINCOLN'S TEAPOT
The symbol of the Society of the
Cincinnati, a fraternity of Revolutionary
officers, decorates this teapot. It is part of
a set of porcelain tableware that bears
the initials "BL," honoring
General Benjamin Lincoln.

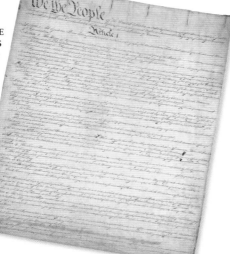

**THE CONSTITUTION OF THE
UNITED STATES**
On September 17, 1787, four
years after the end of the
Revolutionary War,
resentatives of the thirteen
ates met in Philadelphia to
approve an official
nstitution. This document
ablished a federal system
overnment for the states,
and was declared "the
preme law of the land."
American Constitution
ecame one of the most
dmired and influential
cuments in the world.

JAMES MADISON
The cornerstone of the new
American republic was its
Constitution. A key author
of the Constitution was
Virginian James Madison
(1751–1836), considered
an architect of the document,
which created a
government, or federation,
of the newly independent
states. Madison eventually
would become the fourth
President of the United States.

THE UNITED STATES
After the Treaty of 1783
Showing the claims of the older States
to the Western Lands.
The Territory of the Thirteen Original States
after claims had been ceded is tinted.
The Claims to the Western Lands are shown
in border tint of the same color as
the claiming State.
States having no claims are colored thus:

REVOLUTIONARY FINANCIER
Philadelphia merchant Robert Morris
(1734–1806) was an early Patriot
leader who headed the Continental
Congress's Department of Finance
during the war. Morris raised
money and arranged loans to
finance the Revolution, and
afterward helped lay the
foundation for the all-important
financial operations of the new
United States.

A NEW NATION AND ITS CLAIMS
Many of the independent states
claimed ownership of western
lands, but these claims were
eventually turned over to the
federal government. In this map,
claims to western territory are
shown in a tint of the same color as
that of the claiming state.

George Washington—Father of His Country

Early in December 1783, Washington bade farewell to his officers in New York. Among them was General Henry Knox, one of the first to publicly call Washington the "Father of His Country." A few weeks later, Washington resigned his commission before Congress, which was meeting at Annapolis, Maryland. He immediately rode back to Martha and Mount Vernon, but his country soon called again. Washington presided over the 1787 Constitutional Convention in Philadelphia, where he urged that a strong union of the states be established. He served as the first President of the United States, from 1789–1796. The first capital was in New York City and then was changed to Philadelphia—both far from Mount Vernon. Glad to return home after his presidency, he enjoyed the life of a Virginia planter for his last few years. George Washington died at Mount Vernon on December 14, 1799.

WASHINGTON IN VICTORY
Patriot artist Charles Willson Peale created this image of the general a few months after the 1779 liberation of Philadelphia. The painting commemorates Washington's victory at Princeton two years earlier. He posed for Peale in Philadelphia, where the population considered him their greatest hero.

THE GENERAL'S PISTOLS
Washington owned this pair of silver-mounted pistols during the Revolution. They were made in England and bear designs that include the lion and the unicorn. Washington eventually presented them to his private secretary, and nephew, Bartholomew Dandridge.

Silver decoration with the lion and the unicorn

Bidding farewell

After the British evacuated New York City, Washington gathered with his remaining officers on December 4, 1783, at Fraunces Tavern. There, he thanked them for their "glorious and honorable" service. Next, Washington rode to Annapolis, Maryland, to resign as commander in chief. This journey was one long adoring parade; people lined the roads to see him, and balls were held in his honor.

The Fraunces Tavern Museum

Washington's farewell to his officers in Fraunces Tavern.

SIGNING THE CONSTITUTION

Washington was unanimously elected presiding officer of the Constitutional Convention in Philadelphia. He was the one most trusted by the delegates, who were debating bitterly while drawing up the document. On September 28, 1787, as pictured above, the delegates signed the document. In 1789, Washington became the first President of the United States.

STATELY MOUNT VERNON

Washington inherited Mount Vernon from his brother, Lawrence, who built it. When Washington married Martha Custis, who owned several estates, he brought her to Mount Vernon to live. Today, Mount Vernon is a popular place for visitors who wish to learn about the life of an American hero.

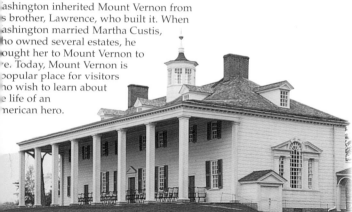

Home at Mount Vernon

While stationed in military headquarters or as the United States president in New York, Washington often longed to be at home with Martha in Mount Vernon. He loved his estate, which overlooked the broad Potomac River, and he was happiest as a hardworking Virginia planter. Washington managed Mount Vernon's agriculture, selected the crops, planned development, and added on to the mansion. The Washingtons were the guardians of two of their grandchildren, who enriched home life at Mount Vernon.

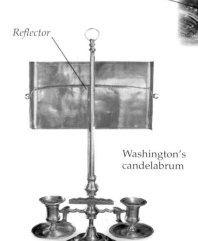

George Washington's grandchildren

THE VIRGINIA PLANTER

Washington enjoyed working on his plantation, overseeing the planting and harvesting of crops. Mount Vernon's fields were tended by slaves, who—in accord with Washington's will—were given their freedom after he and Martha died.

MARTHA CUSTIS WASHINGTON
(1731–1802)

Martha Washington was a devoted wife who shared her husband's joys, sorrows, and duties. Known for her kindness and wisdom, Martha carried herself with the natural style and grace that befitted the first First Lady of the United States.

Reflector

Washington's candelabrum

Porcelain serving dish from Mount Vernon

Index

Acknowledgments

The author and Dorling Kindersley offer their grateful thanks to: Ellen Nanney and Robyn Bissette of the Product Development and Licensing Department of the Smithsonian Institution; Barbara Clark Smith, Jennifer L. Jones, Marko Zlatich, and Lisa Kathleen Graddy of the National Museum of American History, Behring Center; Catherine H. Grosfils, Colonial Williamsburg Foundation; Christopher D. Fox, Fort Ticonderoga Museum; Joan Bacharach and Khaled Bassim, National Park Service, Museum Management Program; Carol Haines, Concord Museum (www.concordmuseum.org); Peter Harrington, Anne S.K. Brown Military Collection; Richard Malley, Connecticut Historical Society; Andrea Ashby, Independence National Historical Park; Claudia Jew, The Mariners' Museum; and Tordis Isselhardt, Images from the Past.

Photography Credits:
t = top; b = bottom; l = left; r = right; c = center
Abby Aldrich Rockefeller Folk Art Museum, Williamsburg, VA: 7tr, 39bl. Adams National Historical Park: 60tl. The American Revolution, by John Fiske: 8tl, 12cl, 13bc, 18cr, 28cr, 31tr, 41bl, 42cl, 44c, 46tr, 47bc, 47br, 54cr, 56bl, 56cr, 57bl, 58tr, 59cr. Anne S.K. Brown Military Collection, Brown University Library: 12bl, 17t,

18tl, 18-19t, 19bl. Boston National Historical Park: 19br. Boston Tea Party Chapter, DAR: 11cl. © David Cain: 8tr, 24bl. Center of Military History, H. Charles McBarron: 24tr, 31bl, 32b, 35br, 55cr, 57t, 59br. The Charleston Museum: 7c, 7cr. The Colonel Charles Waterhouse Historical Museum: 20b, 25b, 36bl, 41t. Colonial Williamsburg Foundation: 7bl, 7br, 10t, 12br, 12tr, 14c, 15c, 23cl, 44cl, 46cr, 48cl, 49bl, 49bc, 49br, 51br, 53tr, 56tr, 61cr. Concord Museum, Concord, Massachusetts: 16tc, 39tr, 59c, 61tr. Connecticut Historical Society: 16bl, 16cl, 19cl, 19tr, 24c, 46tl, 48b, 51tl, 58cl, 59tl. Dahl Taylor: 6tl. Dover Publications: 15tl, 21tr, 31tl, 34b, 42bc, 44bl, 44tl, 46bl. Fort Ticonderoga Museum: 9c, 9cr, 15tc, 17bl, 17br, 17cr, 19c, 22c, 22tr, 46c. © The Frick Collection, New York: 32tl. Independence National Historical Park: 13c, 13cr, 13br, 21cr, 27c, 27bl, 31cl, 36tr, 39tr, 52tr, 55bl. The Institute of Heraldry: 59bl, 59cl (drawing by James Burmester). Library of Congress: 7cl, 8cl, 9br, 10b, 11b, 11tc, 11tr, 12bc, 14bl, 15bc, 15bl, 18b, 19tc, 22b, 23tl, 24br, 26br, 27br, 29b, 29cr, 29tl, 33cl, 34tr, 35bl, 36cr, 38cl, 39tl, 40br, 42bl, 42br, 42tr, 45b, 45cr, 45tr, 47t, 51tr, 53tl, 54tl, 55t, 58b, 59tr, 61bl, 61c, 62br, 63cr. Lexington, Massachusetts Historical Society: 17c, 17cl. Marblehead Historical Society, Marblehead,

MA: 6c. The Mariners' Museum, Newport News, VA: 9t, 38tl, 43t, 43br, 56br. Massachusetts Historical Society: 10cr. Morristown National Historical Park: 44br. Mount Vernon Ladies' Association: 13tl. MPI Archives: 7tl, 40bl, 63cl. National Archives: 16tl, 58tl, 60tr. National Museum of American History: 6bl, 6br, 9cl, 10cl, 15br, 21bl, 25c, 25t, 26c, 29c, 34tl, 39br, 63bc, 63br. National Numismatics Collection: 40cb, 40ct, 43bc, 43bl, 50bl, 50cl. National Park Service: 21cl, 20tr, 31c, 37tr, 37b, 37tc, 53ct. National Park Service, Don Troiani: 20tl, 22cr, 22tl, 23b, 23tc, 35tr, 37tl, 50br, 52-53b, 54bc, 54br. National Park Service, Museum Management Program and Guilford Courthouse National Military Park, photos by Khaled Bassim: 28tr, 28cl, 41c, 45c, 45cl, 45tc, 45tl, 48tr, 49crb, 49crt, 49t, 49tc, 49tr, 50tr, 51bc, 51bl, 52cb, 52ct, 53bl, 53br, 53cb, 55bc, 55br, 57cr, 58ct. National Park Service, Museum Management Program and Valley Forge National Historical Park, photos by Carol Highsmith and Khaled Bassim: 8cr, 9bl, 14cr, 14cr, 15tr, 21br, 21tc, 21tl, 23c, 23cl, 23cr, 29tr, 30r, 31cr, 33tc, 33tl, 35cl, 35cr, 36bc, 36tl, 37cr, 41tr, 47bl, 51crb, 51crt, 54cl, 56cl, 57bc. National Portrait Gallery: 11tl, 13bl, 14tl, 26tr, 33tr, 35tl, 40tl, 41bl, 44cr, 46br, 50tl, 61br, 63bl. Peter Newark's Pictures: 26bl. © Ron Toelke

Associates: 30l, 32tr, 54bl. Smithsonian American Art Museum: 16br, 23tr. Sons of the Revolution in the State of New York, Inc./ Fraunces Tavern® Museum, New York City: 31br, 38-39b, 62bl. State Historical Society of Wisconsin: 8bl. U.S. Capitol: 27t, 33br, 57br, 61tl, 63t. U.S. Senate Collection: 28b, 62tr. ©1996, Virginia Historical Society, Lora Robins Collection of Virginia Art: 13tr. West Point Museum, Photos © Paul Warchol Photography, Inc.: 24cr, 33cr, 33bl, 62c. Winterthur Museum: 60b.

Main cover credits: Colonial Williamsburg Foundation: front bl, front bc. The Connecticut Historical Society: front c. The Mariners' Museum: front cl. National Park Service, Don Troiani: back clb. National Park Service: clt. Smithsonian American Art Museum: front br, back crb. West Point Museum, Photos © Paul Warchol Photography, Inc.: back br, back bl, crt.

Cover credits for top bar images from left to right: Library of Congress: 1st from left. Connecticut Historical Society: 2nd. Smithsonian American Art Museum: 3rd. West Point Museum, Photos © Paul Warchol Photography, Inc.: 4th. Colonial Williamsburg Foundation: 5th. National Portrait Gallery: 6th.

1. BIRD
2. ROCKS & MINERALS
3. SKELETON
4. ARMS & ARMOR
5. TREE
6. POND & RIVER
7. BUTTERFLY & MOTH
8. SPORTS
9. SHELL
10. EARLY HUMANS
11. MAMMAL
12. MUSIC
13. DINOSAUR
14. PLANT
15. SEASHORE
16. FLAG
17. INSECT
18. MONEY
19. FOSSIL
20. FISH
21. CAR
22. FLYING MACHINE
23. ANCIENT EGYPT
24. ANCIENT ROME
25. CRYSTAL & GEM
26. REPTILE
27. INVENTION
28. WEATHER
29. CAT
30. BIBLE LANDS
31. EXPLORER
32. DOG
33. HORSE
34. FILM
35. COSTUME
36. BOAT
37. ANCIENT GREECE
38. VOLCANO & EARTHQUAKE
39. TRAIN
40. SHARK
41. AMPHIBIAN
42. ELEPHANT
43. KNIGHT
44. MUMMY
45. COWBOY
46. WHALE
47. AZTEC, INCA & MAYA
48. BOOK
49. CASTLE
50. VIKING
51. DESERT
52. PREHISTORIC LIFE
53. PYRAMID
54. JUNGLE
55. ANCIENT CHINA
56. ARCHEOLOGY
57. ARCTIC & ANTARCTIC
58. BUILDING
59. PIRATE
60. NORTH AMERICAN INDIAN
61. AFRICA
62. OCEAN
63. BATTLE
64. GORILLA, MONKEY & APE
65. MEDIEVAL LIFE
66. FARM
67. SPY
68. RELIGION
69. EAGLE & BIRDS OF PREY
70. WITCHES & MAGIC-MAKERS
71. SPACE EXPLORATION
72. SHIPWRECK